# BEFORE JOURNALISM SCHOOLS

# BEFORE JOURNALISM SCHOOLS

## How Gilded Age Reporters Learned the Rules

RANDALL S. SUMPTER

UNIVERSITY OF MISSOURI PRESS
Columbia

**The volumes of this series are published through the generous support of the University of Missouri School of Journalism.**


University of Missouri Press, Columbia, Missouri 65211
Printed and bound in the United States of America
 First printing, 2018.

Library of Congress Cataloging-in-Publication Data

Names: Sumpter, Randall S., 1950- author.
Title: Before journalism schools : how Gilded Age reporters learned the rules / by Randall S. Sumpter.
Description: Columbia : University of Missouri Press, 2018. | Series: Journalism in perspective: continuities and disruptions | Includes bibliographical references and index. |
Identifiers: LCCN 2017056127 (print) | LCCN 2018000081 (ebook) | ISBN 9780826274083 (e-book) | ISBN 9780826221599 (hardcover : alk. paper)
Subjects: LCSH: Journalism--United States--History--19th century. | Reporters and reporting--United States--History--19th century.
Classification: LCC PN4864 (ebook) | LCC PN4864 .S87 2018 (print) | DDC 071.309/034--dc23
LC record available at https://lccn.loc.gov/2017056127

∞™ This paper meets the requirements of the American National Standard for Permanence of Paper for Printed Library Materials, Z39.48, 1984.

Typefaces: Grotesk and Minion

## Journalism in Perspective: Continuities and Disruptions

Tim P. Vos, Series Editor

---

Journalism is a central institution in the social, cultural, and political life of communities, nations, and the world. Citizens and leaders rely on the news, information, and analysis that journalists produce, curate, and distribute each day. Their work must be understood in the context of journalism's institutional features, including its roles, ethics, operations, and boundaries. These features are themselves the product of a history emerging through periods of stability and change. The volumes in this series span the history of journalism, and advance thoughtful and theoretically-driven arguments for how journalism can best negotiate the currents of change.

*Dedicated to the members of my family who patiently endured the drafting of this book.*

# Contents

# Acknowledgments

I COULD NOT have completed this book without the aid of librarians and archivists at the Syracuse University Libraries Special Collection Research Center, the Department of Special Collections at the University of Tulsa's McFarlin Library, the Cushing Memorial Library and Archives at Texas A&M University, and the on-line resources made available by the Image of the Journalist in Popular Culture project at the University of Southern California's Annenberg School for Communication. The staffs at these institutions helped to locate primary source materials instrumental in this project's completion. Stephen Bales, the communication and journalism subject specialist for Texas A&M's library system, was particularly helpful.

Funding for an internal faculty fellowship from The Melbern G. Glasscock Center for Humanities Research at Texas A&M University and release time arranged by my department head, Kevin Barge, made it possible to finish writing the draft. Many colleagues also read draft chapters or exchanged ideas with me. It would be impossible to provide a complete list of those contributors, but some merit special mention. My colleague Leroy Dorsey read the entire manuscript and offered valuable insights and corrections. Brian Linn, Texas A&M professor of history, helped me structure the material. Charles Conrad and Patrick Burkart, both professors of communication at A&M, also tutored me in the ways-and-means of book publishing.

Academics always owe a debt to unnamed reviewers, and I wish to acknowledge their contributions in reading my book manuscript and draft articles that were later revised and published in *American Journalism* and *Journalism History*. Those publications provided part of this book's foundation.

Every book manuscript requires a diligent proofreader, and the accolades for performing that task belong to my wife, Nancy.

# Preface

The idea for this book dates from my first job many years ago as a reporter on a metropolitan newspaper. This newspaper was an anachronism—an afternoon daily in a two-newspaper town. Its backshop was equipped with linotype and stereotype machines. It printed on a letterpress. The city room, like city rooms from a bygone era, was draped in cheap cigar and pipe tobacco smoke. Copy boys rushed about, manual typewriters clattered, editors growled, and cub reporters plotted their first scoop while writing endless and unimportant two-paragraph-long column fillers. Beat reporters dictated their stories over the telephone from grungy press rooms to one of three rewrite men. They were the only ones with electric typewriters. It was a wonderful study in chaos that my undergraduate degree in journalism from a solid state university program had not prepared me for. My collegiate training had taught me only the basics of newswork. There was a world of information that I did not know—from the mysteries of writing the delayed lead to the knack for developing sources who knew things, but did not have the authority to discuss them.

I needed a crash course in these subtle arts; I needed teachers, a rare resource in our city room. At least twice, the city editor nearly cashiered me for my ignorance before more experienced reporters or assistant city editors intervened. I survived because I became a sponge, unsystematically soaking up remedial lessons from any and all sources. My experience was much like that of the nineteenth-century reporters and editors that populate this book. Historians have reached some agreement about the genesis of the rules governing newswork in the late nineteenth century, but their understanding of how those rules flowed through Gilded Age journalism is not complete.[1]

This book offers an explanation for how that information spread. It uses a recently promulgated model of interpersonal communication, Communities of Practice (CoPs), as a map or a guide to news worker behavior. The CoP model does not represent a radical departure from other theories or histories of communication, but it does incorporate a flexibility not present in others. Diffusion of innovation, for instance, generally requires an elite opinion leader as a catalyst to move new ideas downward. This is not necessarily so of CoPs, whose originators are indebted in some cases to nineteenth-century French sociologist and jurist Gabriel Tarde. I use evidence from autobiographies, trade and general interest publications, career histories, and fictional accounts to argue that journalistic "knowledge brokers" served as the primary conduits for spreading information about reporting and editing conventions across city (news) rooms. These city rooms functioned as CoPs or loci for sharing and storing occupational knowledge. The knowledge brokers who controlled access to this information were not necessarily drawn from the workplace hierarchy.

Chapter 1 provides the economic and social context for understanding Gilded Age journalism, its practices, and the forces acting upon those practices. The chapter relies extensively on government reports issued as part of the 1880, 1890, and 1900 censuses. Chapter 2 reviews the genesis of the CoP model and other theoretical concepts used in this book to explain the development and spread of newswork rules; Chapter 3 explores the jurisdictional struggle between nineteenth-century journalists and academics to control a dividing line between news and fiction. The knowledge brokers who wrote or spread the growing body of newswork rules are profiled in chapter 4. Those rules reinforced the importance of developing sources from every strata of society, for executing the generic interview as the primary news-gathering tool, and for structuring the results in story form, usually the inverted pyramid. Chapter 5 examines how those rules and others helped novice reporters master the human interest story and its foundation, the interview. Chapter 6 describes how authors of newspaper fiction created imaginary city rooms that provided new reporters with CoPs stocked with role models. In chapter 7, the parallel development of rules governing "delinquent" reportorial behavior is examined. Chapter 8 argues that factors similar to those present in the nineteenth century—economic uncertainty, new technologies, and other factors—have created an environment in which twenty-first-century journalists are reconsidering what stories are important, how they should be obtained, and what format should be used to spread them.

# BEFORE JOURNALISM SCHOOLS

Chapter One

# Introduction

Reflecting on his first full year as a newspaper reporter at four different Texas and Louisiana publications, fourteen-year-old Moses Koenigsberg concluded that he had received virtually "no guidance save the outline of immediate objectives" from his superiors.[1] He had taught himself what he knew about the rules of journalism, and his 1892 self-tutorial had included almost as much about how to break the rules as it did about how to follow them. Koenigsberg certainly had learned one of journalism's universal rules—not to offend "sacred cows"—when he reported for the *San Antonio Times* that court officials routinely raided gambling parlors and bordellos so that they could pay their salaries from the court cost fees paid by defendants. Officials retaliated by charging Koenigsberg, his city editor, and the managing editor with criminal libel. Koenigsberg was fired. He fled the town on an east-bound freight train. Eventually finding his way to the *New Orleans Item*, he learned the useful rule-breaking strategy of "combination" reporting, a method of handling high workloads by alternating assignments with reporters from competing newspapers. The resulting stories were not exclusives, but the participating reporters were spared long work days. Koenigsberg's excursion into combination reporting worked well until his partner suppressed a high-profile rape story. Rather than face his city editor about the missed story, Koenigsberg sought a new job at the *New Orleans Truth*. Koenigsberg would survive to become an important figure in daily journalism, but his earlier problems as an untutored cub reporter were shared by most journalists who began their careers in the final decades of the nineteenth century.

Koenigsberg and his peers had picked a problematic moment to pursue careers in journalism. By the 1890s, the era of hand composition, steam-powered presses, and four- and eight-page dailies had passed in larger cities and was passing in smaller towns. New, but expensive high-speed web perfecting presses, linotypes, and means of quickly reproducing illustrations had arrived, making possible larger daily newspapers attractive to both advertisers and readers. Post-Civil War publishers, however, quickly saturated markets with multiple newspapers and exhausted revenue sources. To cut costs, they needed a way to quickly and cheaply fill the larger newspapers. As part of the solution, they hired inexperienced reporters and did little to train them. These novices needed to be interchangeable and, if possible, mostly self-taught in the steps for finding, gathering, and writing news. Their minimal value to the enterprise meant they could be dismissed in slack periods like the summer months or if their performance was inadequate.

The cub reporters who successfully navigated this harsh environment learned to seek and consult both conventional and unconventional guides to survival. Using a Community of Practice model to organize examples drawn from the lives of more than fifty period reporters, this book explains how newsroom novices accessed multiple sources of instruction to master a core of complex and fluid rules. These resources included multiple "knowledge brokers" and the artifacts they generated in the form of newspaper fiction, guidebooks, face-to-face interactions, periodicals and trade magazines, and the editors who handled the freelance material generated by beginners. Some novices also generated their own newswork rules, like those for finessing a difficult interview. Scholarly research has examined some of these connections between learning opportunities and beginning journalists. More can be learned, particularly about the guidelines for indulging in "delinquent" newswork behavior and their relationship to professionalism. Some of the findings here could be relevant for understanding present-day instances of news delinquency in an economic and technological environment that parallels some aspects of the Gilded Age.

In the late nineteenth century, workers in other occupations shared obstacles similar to those encountered by beginning reporters. Job seekers found the American economy on a roll during the last decades of the nineteenth century, but it had "few rudders or regulations," economist

Scott Derks observed.[2] Between 1865 and 1900, industrialization, immigration, and urbanization were reshaping the business world and the careers of young men and women entering the workforce. The results were not always positive. Before the century ended there would be eight "banking panics." Speculation in rail-line construction and monetary policy caused reverses in 1857, 1873, and 1893 that would contract job markets. The 1873 panic was particularly severe, causing a six-year-long depression.[3] Under such conditions, workers rarely found fulltime employment.[4]

Industrialization of the American economy had begun in the century's early years, but it morphed into "Big Business" in the post-Civil War period with the advent of professional managers and horizontal and vertical integration.[5] The corporation protected by limited liability laws and with access to equity markets replaced partnerships and proprietorships. Inexpensive labor also was available from two sources—agriculture and immigration. In 1870, half the country's labor force of 13 million worked in agriculture; about 16 percent worked in manufacturing. Thirty years later, one-third of the 29 million workers in America were from the agricultural sector and one-fifth were in manufacturing. Overall, immigration and the birthrate increased the country's population from about 40 million in 1870 to 76 million in 1900.

In this business scenario, laborers were easy to replace: "Factory workers, often treated as expendable extensions of the machines they operated, experienced long, sixty-hour work weeks. Working conditions were often deplorable."[6] Unions responded by organizing more than 20,000 strikes between 1880 and 1900, but these had limited success because government entities often intervened on the side of management.[7] Journalism could be counted among the collective bargaining failures. Some journalists believed unions were unnecessary or unworkable. Would-be organizers could not agree whether the proposed institution should be a trade union that taught through an apprenticeship system or a profession learned partly in the classroom. When the American Newspaper Guild finally was launched in 1933, protected in part by the National Industrial Recovery Act, organizers still had not resolved the trade or profession issue. Instead, they opted to refer to journalism as a craft in their planning documents. Journalism, it seemed, required a third, as yet undefined structure for training and disciplining members.

While rank-and-file reporters were not immune to the forces and trends affecting other nineteenth-century workers, publishers also struggled to cope with the changes. Newspaper owners were slow to adopt the new corporate model; it was questionable that their mechanization costs had been offset by savings in labor, and statistics indicated that few markets remained for them to exploit. According to the manufactures report in the Twelfth Census of the United States, only 17 percent of newspapers and periodicals were owned by corporations.[8] Twenty percent were held by partnerships like the one which owned the *New York Sun*, one of the more progressive newspapers. Individuals owned most—about 63 percent—newspapers. This meant only a fraction of news publications could raise cash from equity markets.

The new typesetting, printing, and illustration technologies also were expensive, and some had unintended consequences for publishers. For instance, a trained operator using Ottmar Mergenthaler's mechanical typesetting machine could set roughly the same amount of type in an hour that a hand compositor could in a day. In late 1880s terms, the Mergenthaler machine was expensive and trained operators in larger cities belonged to unions. Publishers could buy one of Mergenthaler's linotypes for $3,000 or lease one for $500 a year.[9] In 1850, workers who set type by hand for New York newspapers earned about nine dollars a week. In 1900, workers who did hand composition earned eighteen dollars a week, but those who could operate a linotype earned even more, according to William Rossiter, who wrote the report on printing and publishing for the Twelfth Census. Speedy typesetting increased the tempo of work elsewhere in the news and press rooms.[10] A new generation of presses added to that work tempo. At the close of 1899, for example, William Randolph Hearst's *New York Journal* installed an R. Hoe & Company press described as "more intricate than any locomotive."[11] It could print 912,000, eight-page, four-color papers per hour. Machines like the *Journal's* new press, which had been an "impossibility in 1880, and an experiment in 1890," were soon in general use at newspapers and inexpensive magazines.[12] Bigger, however, was not always better. For most of the nineteenth century, intermediate-size newspapers had required a press suited to their needs. The Duplex Printing Press Co. introduced a machine in 1884 that could print 3,500 to 4,000 newspaper copies per hour. Further refinement produced a press that could print

5,000 to 5,500 copies per hour of a ten- to twelve-page newspaper. By the turn of the century, more presses of this design operated in the United States than any other.[13]

Rossiter wrote: "It is the opinion of many large employers of labor in this industry that the invention of labor saving machines has merely served to increase the demand for labor in new channels, so that the number of wage-earners employed has actually increased rather than diminished."[14] Technology and questionable policies also produced disappointing results in other areas of publishing.[15] New processes made cheaper, pulp-based paper available during the final decades of the century. In 1900, however, publishers paid 2.3 cents a pound for paper and sold daily newspapers for one or two cents a copy. In New York alone, newspapers paid $2.50 a barrel to purchase a share of the one hundred barrels of paste manufactured daily in the city's six factories.[16] Editors and typesetters used the paste to glue the individual sheets of a story into a continuous roll that was easier to edit and easier to manipulate by linotype operators.

These costs increased the importance of advertising revenue and, consequently, the need to increase circulation. Advertising represented 54.5 percent of newspaper revenue in 1900, 49.6 percent in 1890, and 44 percent in 1880.[17] Rossiter selected the balance sheet of one metropolitan daily, the *Philadelphia Record*, to illustrate these trends over the 1893 to 1900 period. In 1893, about 60 percent of the *Record*'s revenue of $815,474 came from advertising; in 1900, advertising accounted for about 70 percent of its $1.209 million income. Wages and news-gathering costs were the newspaper's largest expense in 1893, about 49 percent of the total, compared with 53 percent seven years later. Industry-wide, advertisers were accumulating immense financial control over newspapers. By 1900, Rossiter found large advertisers were forming combinations to control which newspapers received how many advertising dollars:

> [I]t is said that the patronage of fewer than twenty advertisers forms more than half the total quantity of advertising appearing in the daily newspapers of New York city. The only new source of income in the field of advertising was found in new-comers—principally tobaccos, whiskies, cereals, and books. . . . The professional advertising agent might be termed another cause of loss to the daily paper, to the amount of the commissions

> exacted. Between the opposing perplexities of competition and combinations of the advertisers there has been a decline in the advertising earning power of leading newspapers.[18]

Acquiring the new technologies also required publishers to increase capital investment in their businesses, but that did not necessarily guarantee larger profits. For instance, the average capital investment for periodicals of all types in 1900 was $12,574, an increase of 23 percent from 1890.[19] Meanwhile, average product value climbed less than a percentage point to $14,569. The periodical failure rate, about 10 percent in the 1880 census, climbed to 15 percent in 1890 and to 14 percent in 1900.[20] Circulation increases at 35 percent between 1890 and 1900 did not match the 48 percent gain for the previous ten-year period.[21]

Publishers responded to these conditions in part by controlling the cost of labor. They hired more ill-trained workers like Koenigsberg. These workers would have to learn how to roam the city for stories high in human interest value and obtained through informal interviews with eyewitnesses or by firsthand observation.[22] They also would have to learn how to fit the components of a story into a standardized pattern like the inverted pyramid.[23] The productivity demands on these entry-level reporters at metropolitan dailies, which seemed to swallow larger and larger chunks of news with each passing year, were high. In 1900, Rossiter pointed out that seven New York morning dailies produced Sunday editions aggregating 400 pages.[24] These giant papers included sections of eight, twelve, and sixteen pages devoted to news, literature, advertising, and color comics. Even dailies in smaller cities produced large newspapers on special occasions. For Christmas in 1894, the *Duluth Evening Herald* produced a forty-page newspaper; the *Willimantic (Connecticut) Journal*, fifty-two pages; the *Nashville (Tennessee) Banner*, forty-eight. The *Chicago Inter Ocean* printed a sixty-page anniversary edition; the *San Francisco Examiner* published a 120-page World's Fair edition. "Upon the public the effect of such extensive news gathering was very marked; there was a decided increase in human interest; the world became a great neighborhood," Rossiter wrote.[25] Editors also began to hire women—at first to produce home and fashion stories that would attract more women readers and more advertising income. Daily newspaper publishers also invaded the markets of niche publications by printing specialty news on topics like real estate and banking.

The change in who was hired and how they were treated also can be seen in the census data.[26] Between 1890 and 1900, wage earners employed by periodicals increased 10 percent to 94,604, but total pay declined 1 percent, from $50.82 million to $50.33 million.[27] Men sixteen years of age or older represented 73,653 members of the workforce, about 4.6 percent more than in 1890, but their pay declined 4.3 percent. Meanwhile, more women sixteen years of age or older were employed, up 54.5 percent from 1890 to 14,815 workers in 1900. Their pay increased, too, but their yearly average of $312.40 was about half that earned by men. In 1900, the publishing industry employed 6,136 children under the age of sixteen. Their pay averaged $121.14 a year.

By the 1890s, few forward looking editors and publishers questioned whether women should be engaged in newswork. The question for them was in what capacity should women be employed? For their part, experienced women reporters believed their work to be more difficult than acting, but less taxing than the traditional career choice of teacher.[28] Some women already worked as doctors, ministers, lawyers, and college presidents, but male editors seemed willing to employ women to cover only fashion and home economics, society gossip, and club news.[29] Women could expect to be tolerated, not commended for accomplishing those tasks.[30] This was a slight improvement over the conditions they encountered earlier. In the 1870s, Jeannette L. Gilder, who co-founded *The Critic*, recalled working for "for two years in a newspaper office before I received a cent of pay for my work, and I was glad of the opportunity."[31] If they wanted to avoid more of the same, women should be willing to turn down the editorship of the women's page if and when it was offered and to cling to reporting general news.[32]

There was one other form of high-profile reporting that women could do, but it raised questions about professional ethics, the proper public role for women, and other society-wide questions.[33] Like the *New York World*'s Nellie Bly, women could become "stunt" or "front page girls." Stunt reporting required women reporters to overcome physical challenges while pursuing sensational stories.[34] Typical assignments included throwing themselves in front of street cars, sleeping in paupers' beds, and entering "forbidden dives."[35] Stunt reporting was a form of participatory journalism that could be so dangerous that even the stunt girls found ways to avoid some assignments.[36] Practitioners also had to endure criticism from their contemporaries.[37] They were accused of having an unlimited supply of "cheek" or "gall" and of specializing in "gutter" journalism.[38] "Life with these women was just one stunt, one breach of confidence, one keyhole peep-show after another," wrote one critic.[39]

The market for stunt girl stories and other sensational news items proved finite. Both Rossiter and S. N. D. North, who generated the periodical press report for the Tenth Census, had spotted indications that news publications were nearing the saturation point in many areas. By 1900, 451 daily newspapers were published in the country's fifty largest cities, an average of about nine newspapers per city. By comparison, North had found 389 towns and cities with daily newspapers. Those communities averaged 2.5 dailies. The smallest town with a single daily was Elko, Nevada, with a population of 752. Tombstone, Arizona, with a population of 973, had two dailies.

North noted that the 1870s had "witnessed the rehabilitation of the newspaper press in the southern states, as well as a healthy rate of growth there, and an almost reckless audacity among the pioneer printers of the great and growing West. Even in long and thickly settled states like New York and Massachusetts the increase is quite remarkable, being in the former nearly one-third and in the latter nearly one-half."[40] North estimated that newspaper staff sizes now ranged from a single "practical printer" publishing a weekly to from six to twelve employees at dailies with a circulation of 5,000 to 10,000. Larger dailies might employ up to fifty editorial workers, but that number did not include freelancers. The employment practices in 1880 appeared better, at least for part-time contributors, than those found by Rossiter in 1900. North wrote:

> Much of the work upon our best newspapers is done outside of their offices by trained experts in special topics of comment or discussion, who are paid for their contributions by the piece. It has long been the habit, however, to secure for editorial work men who have education and experience, and are capable of doing the best literary work that money will pay for; and journalists of established reputation receive salaries as generous as are paid in any profession in the United States.[41]

What concerned North, however, was an "overdevelopment" of the weekly press.[42] Weeklies, he wrote, usually appeared in towns soon after the railroads. Many did not survive, but those that did were engaged in "minuter localization" with new publications edging into smaller and correspondingly riskier markets.[43] By 1880 weeklies were published in 2,073 of the nation's 2,605 counties.

Rossiter's later census report also noted declines in the growth rates for several categories of news and general reading publications. Using industry directories, he found a 55.7 percent increase in periodicals of all types between 1880 and 1890. Growth in the next decade was 20 percent. Dailies published in 1900 totaled 2,226, compared with 1,610 in 1890, and 971 in 1880. The respective growth rates were 38.3 percent and 65.8 percent. Weeklies totaled 12,979 in 1900 compared with 10,814 in 1890 and 8,633 in 1880 for respective growth rates of 20 percent and 25.3 percent. The big percentage change was in the semi-weekly category. Those publications soared 228.3 percent between 1890 and 1900 for a total of 637 publications. Rossiter reasoned the big gain in semi-weeklies reflected efforts on the part of weekly editors near cities to fight competition from larger daily newspapers. It was easy enough, he wrote, for a weekly editor to double the number of issues printed with little increase in price to subscribers. Slower growth for monthlies and quarterlies, which usually targeted specialized audiences, also indicated that the dailies, particularly those with large Sunday editions, had "invaded every field of journalism" by now targeting those audiences.[44]

Despite the unsettled industry conditions, young men and women still pursued careers in journalism. One industry trade publication put the number of job seekers at 100,000 in 1889, about 10,000 more than the number of people already employed in the field.[45]

The job applicants had diverse motives. In some cases, their pay was needed to balance their family's or a friend's finances. This reason appeared not only in reporters' occupational memoirs, but in fictional accounts of newswork. For instance, Myles Manning, the hero of Kirk Munroe's newspaper novel, *Under Orders: The Story of a Young Reporter*, withdrew from college after his father was blinded and lost his job. Myles's sister, Kate, also withdrew from Vassar to help support the family as a magazine illustrator. The family home is mortgaged, and one of Myles's former classmates encourages him to try journalism. The classmate tells Myles: "If you must go to work at once why not try journalism? It is hard work, but it pays something from the very start, and that is more than can be said of almost any other business."[46] Elizabeth Garver Jordan's fictional heroine, Ruth Herrick, rescues another woman reporter, Virginia Imboden, who has just been fired by a competing newspaper. Desperate and hungry, Imboden accepts dinner from a stranger. The man then suggests that they take a carriage ride. Herrick intervenes. She offers the woman a place to stay for the night, urges her editor at *The Searchlight* to hire Imoden, and buys the woman's account of her encounter with the "Good Samaritan" for twenty dollars.

Stories from real life were no less urgent and shaped the careers of H. L. Mencken, Henry H. Klein, Augustus Thomas, Kent Cooper, Isaac Marcosson, Irvin S. Cobb, and scores of others. Mencken's father died on a Friday in 1899. The next Monday, Mencken secured an unpaid try-out with the *Baltimore Morning Herald*. He did not secure a paying position until another reporter quit. Klein, who eventually worked as a reporter for several large metropolitan newspapers, emigrated with his family from Hungary in 1881. His mother worked as a scrub woman; his father never earned more than fifteen dollars a week as a tailor. Klein left school at age fourteen to become a peddler. He answered an advertisement in 1895 for a night office boy at the *New York Morning Journal*. For three months, he worked from 6:00 p.m. until 2:00 a.m. at the *Morning Journal* and from 9:00 a.m. to 5:00 p.m. at a real estate office. He eventually became a reporter. American playwright and reporter Thomas came from an influential family. His grandfather had been U.S. consul to Falmouth, Great Britain. His father had been an aide-de-camp to General Zachary Taylor during the Mexican War and later was elected to the Missouri state house. Thomas was a page to the U.S. House of Representatives when his family experienced financial problems. He had to send his salary home. He lived on tips from giving tours of the Capitol Building, obtaining autographs from politicians, filling orders for printed speeches, and drawing caricatures of House members. A series of jobs finally led him to a newspaper position. Cooper, who would become the chief executive officer of the Associated Press, worked for a newspaper before deciding on a career in music. But his father, who had served three terms in the U.S. House of Representatives, secured a reporting position for Cooper on the *Indianapolis Press* in 1899. His father died a short time later, and Cooper vowed to pursue a career in journalism rather than music. Cobb also left school because of family financial trouble.

He earned $1.75 a week writing "items"—the generic term for anything but an obituary—for the Paducah, Kentucky, newspaper. By age nineteen, he was the newspaper's managing editor, but his reckless editing attracted several lawsuits. He was demoted to reporter. By age twenty, he was earning twelve dollars a week. Reverses in his father's finances also forced Marcosson to go to work. The managing editor of the *Louisville Times* gave Marcosson an unpaid reporting position. Another reporter quit, and Marcosson, who had worked without pay for six weeks, got the job. "I became a full-fledged reporter at the age of eighteen, charged with complete responsibility for all the news from dog fights to suicides that happened in the East End," he wrote.[47]

Aspiring novelists and short story writers with better family finances thought of a newsroom apprenticeship as the first step on the ladder to a literary career. Some like Munroe, who specialized in adventure yarns for boys, became prolific and skilled book authors. Others had been interested in reporting and editing since their first encounters with the "hobby press" movement. Before 1867, there were fewer than one hundred of these publications written and printed by adolescents, but that number soared to almost 1,000 after Bostonian Benjamin O. Woods invented and marketed a reliable miniature press.[48] Woods's "Novelty Press," costing a few dollars, was well within the budget of a middle-class family.[49] Imitators were quick to follow.[50] The first page of a typical four-page monthly or semi-monthly produced by amateurs contained short stories, serials, and poetry. Interior pages included editorials, an exchange column, a puzzle or game, and announcements.[51] The final page carried advertisements from local businesses and other amateur publishers. Some of the publications appeared once or twice, but others endured until their editors were young adults. Hobbyists met in 1869 in the home of New York publisher Charles Scribner to form a national association. One of the organizers later wrote: "Amateurs are constantly leaving the ranks for a higher species of journalism—professional. Old amateurs whose day has passed are now engaged on professional sheets, and no doubt fill their positions with honor."[52] Former members worked at newspapers in Cincinnati, Baltimore, and St. Paul. More than twenty years later, the *Washington Post* reported many amateurs still hoped to have careers in journalism and were using their hobby to accumulate the experience needed for a "successful start."[53] Other hobby press publishers and contributors pursued careers writing fiction or distinguished themselves in other pursuits. L. Frank Baum, author of the *Wizard of Oz* books, began his career in Syracuse as an amateur publisher; Jack London contributed some of his early work to an amateur press in San Francisco; Thomas Alva Edison joined an alumni group for ex-publishers years after he published his amateur newspaper. A fifteen-year-old Edison operated his press in a baggage car on a commuter rail line from Port Huron to Detroit.

By 1900, amateurs described themselves as "an institution of young men and women who edit, publish or contribute to miniature newspapers and magazines, for pleasure and intellectual improvement."[54] *Scientific American* had endorsed those goals as early as 1871. It recommended that parents purchase an amateur press to keep their sons off the streets and away from bad companions. Instead, a novelty press would "quicken the boy's mind as well as exercise his fingers—for he must be his own editor; composer as well as compositor; proof reader as well as pressman."[55] Teenagers also could be taught a lesson in economy by running errands and completing other tasks to earn enough money to buy a press.[56] Many would use their new-found knowledge to start boarding school or high school newspapers.

Amateur publishing created two types of readers and writers—either contributors or correspondents. According to Sara Lindey, contributors "used their poems, stories, and letters to break into literary work and develop themselves as professional writers. Correspondents, more often, elicited advice about writing in non-literary professions, imagining themselves as future telegraph operators and clerks and members of the middle-class."[57] Future news workers generally belonged to the contributor category. Nine-year-old Koenigsberg, for instance, ran errands for three months so he could buy type to print his own newspaper. A classmate with a hobby press had interested him in amateur journalism by telling Koenigsberg stories about famous *New York Herald* correspondent Henry M. Stanley. A local job printer donated the press time, but Koenigsberg had to sell advertising to pay for paper and ink. His *The Amateur* began publication in 1888. Koenigsberg applied for membership in a regional association for amateur journalists, but was told only publications that did not accept advertising were eligible. The publisher of a San Antonio newspaper noticed Koenigsberg's work, and he soon had a job at the newspaper. Thomas, the playwright, had his first brush with journalism in a like manner. A friend had a hobby press; Thomas knew how to do etchings. The two decided to publish a magazine. After five issues, however, some readers complained about comments published about them. The magazine folded when the mother of Thomas's friend stopped subsidizing the publication.

Some beginners also thought the life of a reporter would be glamorous, or they underestimated the difficulty of getting their first reporting job. William Salisbury, who began his career in Kansas City, belonged in the former category. As a school boy he shadowed reporters from the four Kansas City newspapers as they covered fires and other news events and spent his spare time in newsrooms. "In my eyes all reporters were heroes, all editors demigods," he wrote.[58] Within nine years of securing his first news job, Salisbury had worked for five newspapers. By then, he was comparing reporters and editors to department store clerks. "I engaged in journalism with the belief that I was entering the noblest profession," Salisbury wrote. "I found American journalism mainly a joke—a hideous joke, it is true, but still a joke—and the joke is on me, and on the immense majority of the American public."[59] Owners considered their newspapers to be just another business; writers and editors considered it to be just another trade, according to Salisbury. Rheta Childe Dorr's experiences were somewhat similar. From her Seattle home, Dorr freelanced stories for East Coast newspapers about the Klondike gold rush. "I haunted the streets, the docks, the outfitting stores, interviewing returned miners, successful and unsuccessful, getting wonderful yarns. Here was material indeed and I knew it," she wrote in her memoir.[60] When she later attempted to get a full-time job with the same newspapers, she learned that journalism not only was demanding, but also a male monopoly.

Finally, newspaper promotions tempted some beginners at an early age. The *Chicago Tribune*, for instance, tried in 1895 a news-gathering experiment involving children. It offered five-, three-, and two-dollar cash prizes to public school students who submitted the best current local news items. It promised to pay six dollars per column for any of the stories that it printed and furnished directions for reporting burglaries, "hold-ups," murders, other crimes, as well as elopements and society-related events. It told youthful readers: "You might hear, though you probably wont [*sic*], of a man eloping with his mother-in-law. Find out the names of both, where they have lived, where they have gone, if they are foolish enough to tell anybody, and send in all the information. Such a story would surely win a prize."[61]

In the long run, the market saturation discovered by Rossiter and North meant even fewer places would exist for a novice to begin a newspaper career. Extraordinary persistence, ingenuity, networking, and physical endurance already were required to get those positions or to move up in the reporting hierarchy. Marcosson was a master at building helpful networks. While assistant city editor at the Louisville newspaper, he also served as book reviewer. He valued this job because through it he met influential writers. Authors would read his reviews, then invite Marcosson to visit them. He had favorably reviewed books by Frank Norris and Ellen Glasgow, leading to friendships with both and pleasing Walter H. Page, editor of *The World's Work* and literary adviser for Doubleday, Page & Co. Norris and Glasgow were Page protégés. Page eventually hired Marcosson.

After failing to get a reporting job in Detroit and being short of funds, Samuel Blythe abandoned most of his luggage, paid a scalper two dollars for a train ticket to London, Ontario, and then walked two weeks through the snow to Buffalo, New York, on the off chance of finding a job.[62] Along the way, he stole food, returning years later to pay for it. Florence Finch Kelly spent four months looking for a job in Chicago. At one point, she spent her last six cents on soda crackers and lived on them for a weekend. She managed to put together a series of part-time jobs, including one proofreading a technical journal at four dollars per week. She did not know how to proofread, but she taught herself with the aid of a dictionary that contained examples of proofreading marks.[63] She eventually got a job at the *Boston Globe*, but the prolonged job search required her, like Marcosson, to make innovative use of book reviews. She worked as an unpaid reviewer for the *Boston Transcript*. The newspaper let her keep the books, which she sold to secondhand stores. Elizabeth L. Banks took an even bigger risk; she tried the London newspaper market. After a few months, she was destitute, but she sold her typewriter for twelve British pounds, replaced it with a machine she bought on the installment plan, and sold her first big story to a London newspaper about the tribulations of maids employed by affluent households.[64]

Charles Edward Russell and a friend tried to get New York reporting jobs during the summer of 1886. The *Herald*, *World*, *Sun*, *Times*, and *Tribune* turned them down. The city editor of the *Commercial Advertiser* told them that most newspapers dismissed staff during the summer. Rather than return home, the two pawned most of their possessions and wrote freelance "sketches, stories, poems, Sunday specials, paragraphs, and (with humiliation I own it) even puns," Russell wrote.[65] Most were rejected. Russell did receive three dollars per week for writing a weekly New York letter for the *Detroit Sunday Tribune.* Just when all seemed lost, an acquaintance told Russell that the *Advertiser* was looking for a reporter. Russell got the job.

The industry's excursion into sensational "yellow" journalism also had ignited an internal debate about legitimate methods for finding, writing, and displaying news stories. This further steepened the learning curve for beginners on probationary try-outs. Their pay already was low; their hours, already long. Benign editors with plenty of time to teach beginners the nuances of the sensational human-interest story did not exist. Universities did not offer degrees in journalism, although some taught a few classes in newswork. Few "how to do journalism" books (also known in the research literature as guidebooks) existed. From the outside looking in, the rules governing newswork appeared to be deceptively complex, falling into several categories. They could vary by geographic region and by market. Some were plainly idiosyncratic like the so-called *index expurgatorius* that editors sometimes tacked to city room walls or the "sacred cows" that beginners had to learn how to placate.

In the 1890s, asking questions about how to do newswork might not be the priority. Journalism was a business, and the relevant question, according to J. Lincoln Steffens, was: "What is the business man going to do with the newspaper?" Steffens asked that question in the first column of an exhaustive examination of journalism published by *Scribner's Magazine* in 1897.[66] To prepare his article, he relied upon his experiences as a reporter and as a newspaper manager as well as interviews with editors, proprietors, and managers of more than one hundred newspapers. Steffens's interview subjects managed newspapers in metropolises like New York, Chicago, Boston, and Philadelphia and in small towns and villages. Newsmen in these markets sold sensation. "If it were something to think about that he [the reader] wanted, the best commodity to offer for sale might be editorials, essays, and important facts. But the commercial journalist, after studying and testing the market, is convinced that his customers prefer something to talk about," Steffens wrote.[67]

As asked by Steffens, whether post-Civil War newspapers should trade in facts or sensations was a commercial question. Broader questions about the principles of written communication including those for news, how to apply those principles, and where to learn them had attracted attention hundreds of years earlier.

Chapter Two

# The Theoreticians

Rules for the written communication of news have been an object of study and instruction since the seventeenth century. Even earlier guidelines had governed the construction of messages for small or specialized audiences. Fifteenth-century English businessmen and government officials learned and followed a set of rules for written communication known as the *ars dictaminis* (art of letter writing). These conventions discussed both form and style and explained in what order business-related news should be revealed to the reader. Writers often violated the *ars dictaminis* except in the case of formal business documents exchanged with Chancery clerks.[1] During the Middle Ages, churchmen produced several treatises for noblemen and their wives on the proper management of large estates and households.[2]

One of the earliest scholarly studies of newspapers and the rules that governed them was a dissertation produced in 1690 at the University of Leipzig by Tobias Peucer. According to media historians, Peucer anticipated "major themes of news research not fully explored until the latter half of the twentieth century."[3] Unlike many researchers that followed, Peucer addressed both the anticipated effects of content and the conventions for its production. Peucer's definition of news incorporated some familiar values—timeliness and significance (or impact). He recommended that the selection of news content should emphasize variety and should entertain readers. Haphazard story structure should be avoided; content should be "immediately intelligible" and use plain, clear language.[4] Accounts should answer what later would be known as the six news questions: Character (or who?), events (or what?), cause (or why?), manner (or how?), place (or where?), and time (or when?). He also suggested standards for ethical newswork. According to Peucer, news should be vetted by contacting sources or confining stories to what the majority of witnesses observed. The resulting accounts should be impartial. He called reporters "collectors of news," but criticized them as "poor historians and an educationally deficient pack of rumor-mongering hacks."[5]

Peucer also produced lists of story categories that appeared or should appear in newspapers and story categories that should never appear. The "never appear" list included stories that affected morals, revealed state secrets, discussed private civil and criminal affairs, and focused on everyday occurrences. Unusual events like floods, changes in government, and ecclesiastical matters did and should appear. Peucer also recommended censorship of newspapers when necessary to protect public morals.

For the most part, nineteenth- and early-twentieth-century researchers who followed Peucer had a different focus. They cared less about the rules for constructing the content of newspapers than they did about that content's effect on audiences. They also had limited interest in building a model of how the rules of newswork circulated through the field. Those questions would not be answered until scholars linked the work of nineteenth-century European theoreticians to present-day research.

A group of Americans known as the "academic muckrakers" dominated the early research on effects.[6] This group included Frances Fenton, Delos F. Wilcox, Alvan A. Tenney, and Byron C. Mathews. All held doctorates, but they borrowed their research assumptions and methodology from John Gilmer Speed, a non-academic. Speed appeared to be the first to use content analysis to evaluate newspapers.[7]

Speed had an axe to grind, and, unlike many press critics of the 1890s, he used numbers rather than anecdotes to make his point. Born in 1853, he held a university degree in civil engineering and came from a prosperous Louisville family.[8] Speed worked as an engineer for several railroads and his hometown before he joined the *New York World*'s staff in 1877 as a correspondent. By 1879, he was the managing editor. Speed remained with the newspaper until Joseph Pulitzer purchased it in 1883. Speed soon left and began a career as a book author, magazine contributor, and magazine editor. Ten years later, Speed's newspaper content analysis was one of three newspaper-related articles published in the August 1893

*Forum*. The other contributors were Charles R. Miller, editor-in-chief of the *New York Times* and president of the Times Publishing Company, and J. W. Keller of the *New York Recorder*. Miller defended some "new journalism" practices that thrived on sensational human-interest stories.[9] Keller condemned editors for manipulating reporters.[10] Speed's article was sandwiched between the two.

Speed's contribution incorporated two assumptions. First, he believed that new journalism had negative effects on readers. If exposed often enough to this content, readers might mimic the negative behaviors that they read about. His second assumption was a Gresham's Law–like rule for news. Rather than "a bad money drives out good" statement, new journalism-style content was displacing serious news that citizens needed to participate in a democratic society. He used his analysis to demonstrate how salacious content had grown by comparing four New York dailies published on April 17, 1881, and April 16, 1893. Speed's claim that he had randomly selected for analysis those Sunday editions of the *Times*, *Tribune*, *Sun*, and *World* served an ulterior purpose. Selecting those dates let Speed compare content that he had edited at the *World* with material produced by a Pulitzer staff. Speed assigned the content of the four newspapers to thirteen categories, but he provided no definitions for his classifications, which sometimes overlapped. His unit of analysis, the newspaper column, also was problematic. The *World* used a seven-column page format in 1881, but changed to eight by 1893. The *Tribune* used six columns during both years, but the *Times* and *Sun* used seven. Speed found that newspaper size had nearly tripled since the ten-page 1881 average.[11] Two content categories—"gossip" and "scandal"—dominated the additional columns. The *World* and *Times* also printed fewer editorials.[12] News about crime and criminals, infrequently used in 1881, according to Speed's coding scheme, now appeared in the *Tribune*, *World*, and *Times*.

He concluded that readers had not benefited from the expansion in newspaper size, but they could be harmed. Speed wrote that news of "serious happenings" was being displaced by stories that promoted "disjointed thinking."[13] Speed's *Forum* article, however, drew little interest. Editorialists at the four newspapers did not comment on it.[14] The August 16, 1893, issue of *Dial* briefly mentioned Speed's work.[15] A trade journal reprinted Keller's piece and later commented that while it was the most significant of the three *Forum* articles, it was unduly pessimistic.[16]

Speed's later academic imitators agreed with his basic assumptions about content: Sensational stories could not only negatively influence reader behavior, but they could also crowd out useful and accurate information. Newspapers, like schools, had to perform properly if a democracy were to thrive. In the course of their work with content analysis, the muckraker academics found few newspapers that served those needs. Like Speed, they had little interest in how content was created or how professionalization of the press corps might eliminate the problems represented by the new journalism. After reviewing the literature, Fenton, a University of Chicago fellow, concluded newspapers primarily organized gossip for readers.[17] Wilcox, a civic reformer who believed a newspaper's duty was to control the state through the publication of facts, found that content was dominated by "petty excitements."[18] Tenney, a Columbia University sociologist, believed a series of improved content analyses could chart the "social weather" in America.[19] Tenney, however, reported his 1912 trial of Speed's method did not produce interpretable results. Part of the reason, Tenney believed, involved the difficulty he encountered in defining news and in consistently assigning items to the seven-category coding scheme he had developed. Mathews, a public school administrator, reported similar problems.

The points made by Speed and his imitators were not too different from those incorporated later in mass society theory. This theoretical perspective incorporated some key assumptions about the press and society. They included the belief that newspapers were a powerful force that could threaten or enhance social order.[20] Later essays by University of Chicago sociologist Robert Ezra Park began to address questions about the process of newswork, not just the outcome. Park grouped his conclusions about the press under a theory of competition and communication. Briefly summarized, Park believed forms of communication integrated society while forms of competition "individuated" its components. He believed that expanding the definition of news to attract more readers increased newspapers' political power because news, not editorials, which were disappearing from newspapers, drove opinion formation in American society. At the outset of his work, Park considered news and communication to be fresh terrain for study. He wrote in 1923: "As a matter of fact we do not know much about the newspaper. It has never been studied."[21] His chief observations about news and communication are scattered throughout a number of scholarly publications, but his main points were: 1) News circulates as far as audiences find it interesting and intelligible, 2) American editors and reporters produce content that is easy to read, and 3) Not everything that appears in a newspaper is news. Park noted: "Much that is printed as news is read, at least, as if it were literature; read, that is to say, because it is thrilling and stirs the imagination and not because its message is urgent and demands action. Such, for example, are the 'human interest' stories, so called, which have been so influential in expanding and maintaining newspaper circulation."[22]

The "news" story and the "fiction" story had become so much alike that they could not be distinguished from one another. "New journalism" and its "yellow" variation had discovered the perfect content formula for urban readers—stories of love and romance for women readers and accounts of sports and politics for the men.[23] Park had limited interest in the conventions that controlled actual newswork, but his research earned him the reputation as the founder of media sociology.[24] More focused inquiries into news conventions or the rules for finding, obtaining, and writing the news did not appear until the 1930s. These early studies included Gordon Allport and Janet M. Faden's 1940 "newspaper psychology" study, Leo C. Rosten's 1935–1936 survey of Washington correspondents, Francis Prugger's investigation in 1941 of the backgrounds, opinions, and attitudes of reporters at a Midwest daily; Charles E. Swanson's 1949 "control" analysis of news workers and readers, and David Manning White's 1950 "Mr. Gates" study.[25]

This research line eventually produced book-length, ethnography-based studies like those produced by Gaye Tuchman,[26] Mark Fishman,[27] and Phyllis C. Kaniss.[28] Those works focused on how reporters, editors, and producers did their work, less on how they learned particular occupational skills.

The academic muckrakers and even some later, more sophisticated researchers had not produced a model that explained how beginners learned and circulated newswork rules through nineteenth-century city rooms and other work groups. Ideas for this model would be suggested by the work of European theoreticians like Emile Durkheim, Gabriel Tarde, Gustave Le Bon, and Graham Wallas. Contributions from Tarde, a French sociologist and jurist, would be particularly important. Tarde referred to the nineteenth century as the age of invention for both the physical and social sciences. He predicted that it would take another one hundred years to understand these discoveries and their place in the social world. The large, metropolitan newspaper counted as one of those inventions, and Tarde's work provided a foundation for understanding how information flowed through news organizations. For Tarde, the interesting phenomenon was interpersonal communication, not mass communication.[29] The three central concepts in the Tarde model of the social world were invention, imitation, and opposition. An American editor of Tarde's papers offered this synopsis of the relationship among the three: "Inventions, the creations of talented individuals, are disseminated throughout social systems by the process of imitation. These imitations spread—to use one of Tarde's favorite analogies—like the ripples on the surface of a pond, regularly progressing toward the limits of the system until they come into contact with some obstacle."[30]

The likely obstacle was an imitation of an earlier invention. Tarde used a broad definition of invention. An invention could be an idea, a physical construct like the wheel, or a change in a routine for conducting diplomacy. Imitation occurs first near the site of an invention, then spreads like Tardean "ripples." This process can replicate itself in both small groups and in large organizations and institutions. The knowledge used to create new inventions also is cumulative with old knowledge providing a foundation for new creations. High-density communication networks encourage invention; the greater the isolation of a society or an individual, the lower the level of inventiveness. Inventions similar to those already being imitated are likely to be more readily accepted or incorporated into a social unit. According to Tarde, invention and imitation usually spread downwards from elite sources, but that is not always the case. Superior inventions take the place of inferior solutions regardless of their origins. Inventions usually spread throughout a social system as soon as elites legitimize them by adopting their use. Tarde's editor called this process a "pump priming effect."[31] Tarde's system is reminiscent of the "observation and imitation" approach novice nineteenth-century news workers reported using in an attempt to learn from editors and accomplished reporters. The spread of "news" inventions, like human interest stories, through high-density communication networks like newsrooms, also are suggested by his model.

Twentieth-century researchers have produced two explanations for how Tarde-like "inventions" move through an organization or an institution—diffusion of innovation or information and communities of practice (CoPs). Diffusion inspired studies have been used in the past by researchers to explain the spread of information or innovations; CoP-based explanations have only recently been employed.

Everett M. Rogers borrowed directly from Tarde's work to build his diffusion of innovations theory.[32] Like Tarde, Rogers, an Ohio State University sociologist, employed a very broad definition of his key concept:

> An innovation is an idea, practice, or object that is perceived as new by an individual or other unit of adoption. It matters little, so far as human behavior is concerned, whether or not an idea is "objectively" new as measured by the lapse of time since its first use or discovery. The perceived newness of the idea for the individual determines his or her reaction to it. If an idea seems new to the individual, it is an innovation.[33]

Textbook authors have added technologies, neologisms, objects, behavioral codes, and beliefs to the list of items that can move through a group or between groups through the process of diffusion.[34] Diffusion of an innovation or information moves through discrete stages: awareness, interest, evaluation, trial, and adoption, but the progression is not necessarily linear. It involves "cycles of divergent and convergent activities that may repeat over time and at different organizational levels" provided that resources are available to renew the cycle.[35]

Diffusion or diffusion-related studies have been used before to explain the appearance of media content codes or canons, the spread of or change in news-gathering routines, and the interpretation of nineteenth-century circulation numbers. Working from a diffusion curve developed by Melvin DeFleur that plotted maximum penetration of an audience as one newspaper subscription per household, John Dimmick determined that media developed content codes within a few years of reaching their maximum, heterogeneous audience. Newspapers, for instance, reached the one-subscription per household threshold in about 1904. Within nine years, the American Society of Newspaper Editors drafted the Canons of Journalism. Dimmick concluded that: "A definite pattern is apparent; as the medium attains universal acceptance, it becomes vulnerable to criticism from an increasingly diverse audience and must form a code to demonstrate its social responsibility."[36] He demonstrated the same relationship between audiences and content codes for radio, television, and movies.

Others have used ideas from diffusion theory to study the spread of the inverted pyramid story format in the late 1800s. Other factors contributing to increased readership that developed at the same time included reduction in story length, use of illustrations and headlines, and dividing newspapers into topical sections. Diffusion of the inverted pyramid—or "top-heavy form"—was rapid, but according to some research it occurred later than generally thought. Researchers studying the content of the *New York Herald*, known for news innovations in post-Civil War America, and the *New York Times* found the inverted pyramid structure appeared no earlier than 1875 or later than 1895.[37] Earlier research indicated this change occurred alongside the use of the telegraph at mid-century and accelerated with the demand for news during the Civil War. Michael Schudson found a similar diffusion of routines between 1790 and 1900 in how the press reported the State of the Union Address.[38]

Diffusion concepts also have been used to understand newspaper circulation rates in the late nineteenth century. Rather than use circulation rates per capita that included children and rural readers, for instance, Ted Curtis Smythe used a more accurate per urban household rate to study how newspapers had penetrated American society. He found that newspapers sold 2.61 copies per urban dwelling in 1900, the highest rate for both the nineteenth and twentieth centuries.[39] Smythe concluded that traditional explanations for gains in circulation—the publication of evening newspapers using the new journalism formula, urban annexation, immigration, and other factors—were insufficient. Advances in transportation systems that linked urban worksites to suburban homes played a part. Commuters were reading some of the additional newspapers; the same transportation systems also made cheap delivery to suburban subscribers possible.

Diffusion, however, generally is used to explain how knowledge or innovations move through an audience, not how people learn or master that knowledge. The CoP model addresses the "how" question. Borrowing from the theory of structuration developed by British sociologist Anthony Giddens, researchers at the Institute for Research on Learning in

Palo Alto, California, developed the CoP model in the 1990s.[40] The Palo Alto scholars primarily were interested in understanding how organizations managed knowledge. Since then, other research communities have found the CoP model's "loose" conceptualizations of "community" and "practice" to be both a benefit because they contribute to the theory's reusability and a flaw because of their ambiguity.[41]

CoPs are sometimes described as "containers" to store work and life competencies.[42] Those contributing to these containers share three common attributes: Mutual engagement (the level of communication and interaction among members), joint enterprise (a common set of tasks that group members perform and can influence), and a shared repertoire for completing these tasks.[43] This repertoire, or collection of work-related artifacts, includes "routines, words, tools, ways of doing things, stories, gestures, symbols, genres, actions, or concepts" that community members have produced or have adopted.[44] CoPs often emerge spontaneously to cope with a new problem encountered by an occupation, like those confronting news workers today or in the past.[45] They function informally, not responding to deadlines or to workplace hierarchies.[46] Each CoP has its own boundaries, and a bridge must be provided if knowledge is to spread through multiple CoPs. Once connected, these larger social units are equivalent to "constellations" of interrelated CoPs.[47]

Ethnographers have determined that "knowledge brokers" provide the bridges to interconnect individual CoPs.[48] These brokers can cross boundaries to introduce new ideas and practices to CoPs or to reaffirm existing rules and routines. To be effective, however, brokers have to be perceived as accomplished and authoritative practitioners coming from far enough away—either intellectually or physically—that their contributions will be considered as genuinely new.[49] Part of a knowledge broker's task is to spread "boundary objects" like the work artifacts described earlier.[50] Knowledge brokers also can adopt three roles: As boundary spanners who over time maintain borders among groups, as roamers who move knowledge from place to place, and as outposts that explore new areas and fetch back fresh artifacts from them.[51]

CoP and information or innovation diffusion models share parallels. Diffusion theory's change agents, who shepherd innovations through their evolution from awareness to adoption, are similar to CoP's knowledge brokers. As originally promulgated, however, diffusion theory depended upon a medium to initially engage the interest of potential innovators or users of new information. Diffusion theory also is a top-down model of human behavior. An "elite" or central source begins the interaction. Some of the knowledge brokers studied here would not qualify as elite sources in the same sense as Rogers's. The CoP model also is not necessarily dependent upon a mass medium to function properly. It thrives within small audiences and higher quality person-to-person relationships that probably do not exceed 150 workplace connections.[52]

Despite recent interest, the CoP model and its knowledge brokers likely represent what Heather Smith and James McKeen called a new name for an old social mechanism.[53] Their insight suggests CoPs may offer a fresh, but legitimate way to look at the spread through *fin de siècle* newsrooms of journalistic rules and routines.

Although media historians have reached some agreement about the genesis of nineteenth-century work standards, their understanding of the rules' spread through newsrooms and their consequences for news workers is not complete. The focus here is on the standards as reporters learned them, how those rules moved through their occupational lives, and how they responded. There still is much to learn about nineteenth-century newswork. The problem in part exists because media history has not produced a universally accepted conceptualization of work standards, conventions, or other similar words. The "loose" conceptualizations used in CoP literature eventually could prove helpful here. Media historians now use a variety of conceptualizations for news standards that reflect different research goals or even variations in the primary source materials used.[54] Hazel Dicken-Garcia developed one of the more flexible definitions. She defined "standards" as "the criteria, or rules of procedure, governing the accomplishment of an occupational end—those 'rules,' for example, that define how information is to be collected, incorporated into a report, and presented in published form."[55] Dicken-Garcia argued that these work routines should not be confused with moral principles that guide behavior in large social units or be confused with codes of occupational ethics.[56] In a later study of nineteenth-century and early twentieth-century trade journal content, Patrick Plaisance used a similar approach to differentiate ethical values and professional standards. He defined standards as the "time-specific ideas and concepts that, on a practical basis, are used to guide daily conduct."[57] Defined in this manner, journalistic standards can be considered another form of press technology developed and applied because of a number of concrete factors like economics, an approach used by Patricia Dooley.[58]

The terms "rules," "standards," and "conventions" are used interchangeably in this book, but the reporters and editors that populated the late nineteenth century had a preference. They frequently used the word "rule," but they often inflected the meaning by adding an adjective. Some rules were fixed; others, not.[59] There were "excellent" rules to follow.[60] Irvin Cobb referred to "academic" rules, implying that some dicta could not or would not be followed.[61] Charles Edward Russell split rules into "traditional" and "temporary" categories.[62] Presumably, the temporary category would receive less attention after some point in time. In other cases, particularly in "how-to-do-it" publications (also known as guidebooks in the research literature), authors would use a phrase. Examples are: "points on which uniformity is desirable,"[63] a "professional secret,"[64] and rules that to "follow blindly" might cause harm.[65] One guidebook published in the early post-Civil War period made no mention of rules. The anonymous author referred instead to "suggestions." He or she explained: "Practice alone will give real instruction. The comparison of subjects to determine their value, the preparation of news, and that quick comprehension of the meaning and importance of subjects by which they can receive immediate discussion and comments—all these can be successfully mastered only by experience."[66] What label was applied to the skills and principles used by reporters and editors apparently mattered little to journalism's practitioners.

What did matter as the nineteenth century closed was whether journalists could fashion an identity with borders, artifacts, and knowledge brokers like other occupations.[67] Would this constellation of CoPs be a trade, a craft, or a profession?

Before the Civil War, law, religion, and medicine were considered to be the professions. Postwar industrialization created new occupations like engineering, accounting, and architecture that sought professional status.[68] The result was a "culture" of professionalism that swept the nation and that valued practitioners with university degrees. These new professions thrived on "an atmosphere of constant crisis—emergency—in which practitioners both created work for themselves and reinforced their authority by intimidating clients."[69] Editors and reporters, who used the new journalism formula to exaggerate the importance of news events, real or imagined, were an example of this phenomenon.[70] But understanding the rules for the new journalism was not enough to claim professional status. Professions exist as specialized communities within a larger society. These communities within a community shared other, common traits. In a review of the related research published between 1914 and 1957, William J. Goode found eight of these commonly held characteristics.[71] They were: 1) a shared identity among practitioners, 2) permanent employment once training was completed, 3) shared values, 4) a role definition shared by both members and non-members, 5) a common work language understood only in part by non-members, 6) a community ability to sanction members, 7) clear social boundaries with others, and 8) control over the selection and training of new community members. A later study produced a shorter and more manageable list that included serving the needs of clients first and the development of a code of ethics.[72]

Goode and others argued that professional identity was based on sharing some or all of those traits. Others like Andrew Delano Abbott and Dooley claimed there was a simpler standard. Abbott wrote that competition among professions for jurisdiction over a particular body of knowledge or collection of tasks better determined membership in an occupational group.[73] Abbott used journalism as an example. Journalism, he wrote, belonged to the information professions, a group that could be divided into qualitative and quantitative categories. Journalism belonged in the qualitative category along with librarians, academics, advertisers, and others. Demand for fact-based stories during the Civil War caused journalists to abandon their earlier jurisdictional claim over providing entertainment to readers with material like the hoaxes published in the Penny Press era. Instead, journalism shifted its jurisdictional claim to providing fact-based stories. Journalism's authority over this occupational task grew, but not without continuing conflicts over the borders between it and public relations, according to Abbott. Abbott believed these jurisdictional battles often began with the appearance of "a disturbance—a new technology requiring professional judgment or a new technique for old professional work."[74] Journalism, with its new technologies and story format innovations, experienced those "disturbances" during the last quarter of the nineteenth century. Dooley likewise argued that for most of the nineteenth century, journalists were locked in a struggle with political parties about jurisdiction over political news and ideas.[75]

When compared to Goode's list of attributes, nineteenth-century journalism could not claim to have mastered many. The traditional professions, however, had not mastered them all, either. At the beginning of the twentieth century only 10 to 12 percent of doctors, 15 to 20 percent of lawyers, and 33 percent of Protestant clergy held university degrees.[76] Journalism, however, fell short in several categories. Reporters and editors could not always place the readers, their clients, first. A university education was not required, and members of the journalistic community could not impose formal sanctions on its members, although informal methods existed and were used.

Educators considered journalism to be "a troubled profession" that would benefit from specialized university training, but progress in this area was only beginning to be made.[77] Until the twentieth century, most journalists reputedly learned their trade through long, but sometimes ineffective apprenticeships.[78] Though taxing, these news apprenticeships probably were no more onerous than those endured by men and women seeking training in other occupations.[79] Not counting course work devoted mostly to type-setting, American universities did not offer a sequence of journalism courses until 1893. That year, the University of Pennsylvania's Wharton School of Business introduced a five-course curriculum taught by a news professional.[80] Course work included the history of the press, business practices and libel law, a three-hour practicum, lectures on current press issues, and attendance at public lectures given by working professionals. The first separate school of journalism was founded fifteen years later at the University of Missouri.

Some editors and experienced reporters believed exposure to a university-level liberal arts education might benefit new reporters, but the complexities of newswork could only be learned in a newsroom.[81] Articles in general interest and trade publications more often than not discouraged job seekers. These articles portrayed journalism as an "outsider" profession or a profession of the last resort.[82] The preface to E. L. Shuman's *Steps Into Journalism: Helps and Hints for Young Writers*, a nineteenth-century guidebook to newswork, captured the tone:

> It is not the aim of this book to make any more writers: we have too many now. On none of these pages will there be found a single word tempting any young man to leave the farm or the business office, or advising any young woman to forsake the household routine, in order to run after the *ignis fatuus* of literary fame. Where there are words of encouragement or enthusiasm they are for those only who have the divine call—which, in preacher and editor alike, is nothing but the native ability to do that one thing better than any other thing in the world.[83]

The year before publication of *Steps Into Journalism*, J. W. Keller, who served a term as president of the New York Press Club, warned those considering a career as reporters that journalists represented an unorganized labor pool that routinely was exploited by capital.[84] Another contributor to a trade journal warned that a reporter's work was not governed by "a regular, uniform science of rules and conduct, controlling all journals alike."[85] No fixed doctrine existed that could be taught in the classroom.[86] Any new reporter must spend some time learning how the game was played at each fresh newspaper assignment. A career in journalism did have some advantages. The occupation required little or no start-up capital. Novices could pursue it at any time.[87] The effort required to succeed in journalism was comparable to that in other professions.[88] Shuman insisted: "Most newspaper readers do not realize that journalism has grown to be a profession requiring every whit as hard study and preparation as medicine or the law—that it is no easier to become a great editor than to attain distinction as a famous professor."[89]

Without college courses, textbooks, and willing mentors, young reporters had to rely in part upon books like *Steps Into Journalism* and trade magazines to learn the rules and skills that were exclusively the jurisdiction of journalism.[90] Trade journals, also known as industrial, class, or business papers, proliferated with post-war industrialization. Not only did readers use them as textbooks, they also used them as forums to discuss standard practices as well as new processes or solutions.[91] By the 1890s, business papers existed for electricians, architects, dry goods retailers, druggists, jewelers, exporters, harness makers, paper and press manufacturers, haberdashers, and many more industries and businesses. Their publishers had created several national, regional, and local organizations including the American Trade Press Association, the

Associated Trade Press Association, the Southern Trade Press Association, and the Chicago Publishers' Association. These organizations considered reform of business practices to be a priority.[92] The activities of trade press publishers also received scrutiny. At a meeting of the American Trade Press Association, members debated whether they should sanction members who took goods in lieu of cash payment for advertising.[93] The Chicago association considered whether members should participate in politics.[94] Several trade papers served different facets of the newspaper industry, but they were not mouthpieces for professional associations. In New York, for instance, *The Journalist*, founded by Allan Forman and two partners, offered content meant for newsroom employees.[95] Forman's rivals were *Newspaperdom*, *Fourth Estate*, and *Editor & Publisher*.[96] *Newspaperdom* appeared in 1892 and provided content for publishers of small dailies and weeklies. *Fourth Estate*, which began publication in 1894, featured material for business managers and the superintendents of mechanical departments. *Editor & Publisher* did not appear until 1901, but it eventually absorbed the other three periodicals. Like other businesses, the journalism trade press served as a nexus for the discussion of professionalism and ethical behavior, even though their content often referred to journalism as a "respectable trade."[97]

However they mastered it, nineteenth-century cub reporters faced a complex "curriculum." Present-day researchers tend to divide it into two parts—news values and news routines. News values are the traditional list of attributes that permit news workers to gauge a person's or event's newsworthiness, and news routines structure how news is obtained.[98] Other divisions have been used. David Ryfe divided newswork into activities or concepts that were governed by constitutive and regulative rules. "Where constitutive rules tell us what the news is, regulative rules tell us how the news ought to be produced," he wrote.[99] Some of these rules were explicit, others implicit.[100] Organizational communication scholars described routines (or rules) and their associated skill packages as repeated patterns of interdependent behavior that serve as knowledge storehouses.[101] Those storehouses could include guidelines for deviating from workplace rules when necessary to complete a task. Acts of workplace deviance also could "strengthen group solidarity, teach group expectations, and reinforce group values."[102] For instance, some forms of research malpractice are common among scientists.[103] In the nineteenth century, competition among newspapers, the individual's desire to be first with a story, and changing news values likewise contributed to the bending of rules within news CoPs.[104] News workers from that era, however, did not speak in terms of routines or a dichotomy, nor did they frequently talk about a behavior code. They seldom referred to their work as a profession.[105]

Cub reporters who began journalism careers in the last quarter of the nineteenth century encountered the sort of complex and fluid environment described by Abbott. New technologies and techniques had to be mastered if journalism was to maintain its jurisdiction over news. The apprenticeship system for teaching cubs could not efficiently transmit both the old and new rules to beginners. Other knowledge brokers had to be enlisted, and cubs found them in works of newspaper fiction, autobiographies written by experienced reporters, and other sources examined in this book. These artifacts and their custodians formed CoPs capable of defining news and related concepts, of explaining how news could be collected, and of describing how it should be written. Where autobiographies are used in this book as evidence, the author followed the guidelines developed by other historians for the interpretation of these "occupational" memoirs. Their authors likely were atypically successful journalists who influenced newswork with idealized accounts of their conduct.[106] Their autobiographies have been used here to uncover shared life and work patterns and their attitudes and beliefs about journalistic work.[107] After reflection, these authors have shared their ideas for the best training of reporters and have outlined rules for everything from interviewing sources to covering wars.[108] Whether and how fiction can be used as a primary source in historiography is a continuing debate among historians. Some, like Booker Prize winner Penelope Fitzgerald, argue that historians should not limit their work to fragments of objective evidence. To do so limits their ability to explain why some events happened and excludes legitimate speculation about unrecorded events.[109] Subjective narratives, like those produced by the journalists turned fiction writers studied here, can create and deepen historical understanding without misleading.[110] This book employs that argument.

## Chapter Three

# The News Debate

THE NEW, BUT expendable reporters infiltrating city rooms eventually learned to consult the knowledge brokers that populated disbursed CoPs built around books, trade journals, and other sources. They also learned that the experienced news workers who produced those artifacts did not necessarily share the same nomenclature or define concepts in the same manner. The discrepancies reflected in part jurisdictional conflicts with other occupations.

For example, nineteenth-century reporters did not consistently define journalism as a profession. "Craft" and "trade" often were used instead. Allan Forman, editor of *The Journalist*, thought of journalism as a "respectable trade."[1] In her autobiography, Rheta Childe Dorr recalled hearing the opposite from an editor that she hoped would hire her. During the course of his interview with Dorr, he called journalism an "accursed trade."[2] Moses Koenigsberg complained that during the course of the 1890s, journalism had been transformed from a professional service to a complicated manufacturing business.[3] William Salisbury thought he was entering "the noblest profession" but found it a joke. "Journalism in America is, in nearly every case, but a business to newspaper owners and managers, and a trade to writers and editors," he wrote.[4] Others wrote that the absence of bylines ensured the reporter would remain an anonymous cog in publishing.[5]

Knowledge brokers also critiqued the occupation's chief commodity, news. The sensational and exaggerated content of "yellow journalism," according to Julian Ralph, belonged in a circus. Reporters not yet seduced by sensationalism should keep two things in mind—getting the stories they were assigned to pursue and keeping their hands clean and their minds open in the process.[6]

Journalism was perhaps one of the few occupations that delighted in public doses of self-criticism, particularly when humorous. Ray Stannard Baker recounted in his autobiography overhearing Arthur Brisbane, who had been a highly praised managing editor for the *New York World* before joining William Randolph Hearst's organization, impart this advice to a reporter: "If you would succeed in journalism, never lose your superficiality."[7] While covering the 1905 negotiations to end the Russo-Japanese War, Will Irwin and Irvin S. Cobb noticed a colleague wore the Order of St. Stanislaus, a decoration awarded by the Russian empire. Wearing the medal indicated that something other than unbiased reporting could be expected. Irwin and Cobb quickly invented the fictitious Order of St. Vitus of Crete. Those "earning" the award would wear in a buttonhole "a bow of white ribbon representing the innocent public, bound at the center with a narrow strip of yellow symbolizing the anaconda coils of the sensational reporter."[8] In his work memoir, Salisbury included Otto von Bismarck's definition of a reporter: "One who has failed in his profession."[9]

If there was some confusion within the ranks of journalism about professionalism and related concepts, it was confusion shared with university English professors. They debated where the boundary between literature and news should be drawn. Occupations build their identities in part by controlling a distinct work-related nomenclature and their ability to define key, work-related concepts.[10] Controlling the definition of "news" was a key component of *fin de siècle* journalism's identity because it established the occupation's apartness from other jobs, particularly the text-based work of playwrights, poets, and novelists. News, however, was difficult to define. Its definition seemed to be score-able on a variety of scales including the passage of time. The words "reporter" and "editor" were seldom mentioned in these definitions, but "reader" and "audience" as clients were. Sorting out a definition, however, was a necessary step in the delineation of newswork from other occupations, particularly literary work where there were similarities.

Both literature and journalism told stories—one, fact based; the other, based on fiction. In the nineteenth century, it was not uncommon for novelists and short story writers to complete an apprenticeship first in newspaper writing. A partial list by a present-day researcher of those who had survived these apprenticeships includes Mark Twain, William

Dean Howells, Stephen Crane, Willa Cather, Frank Norris, Jack London, Henry James, Bret Harte, Ambrose Bierce, and others.[11] The narrative text generated by news interviews was like the dialogue and description in a play. The "color" used to enliven an interview with an important public figure was much like that used to develop characters in a novel or short story. Under these circumstances, some preferred to think of journalism as part of the "broader profession of authorship."[12]

Differences also existed between news and other types of narratives. Historian Mitchell Stephens summarized them: "Historical data usually lack the requisite freshness to qualify as news; art, for the most part, does not offer that layer of compelling information; government intelligence is reserved for private use; chitchat often is of only personal interest—though in small communities, with smaller publics, reports on family or friends often are newsworthy."[13] Mark Canada offered this comparison: Journalism offers timely facts in a format for mass audiences; literature uses artistic ways to explore timeless truths for select readers.[14] Journalism also used a space-saving approach to diction and syntax not employed by fiction. The end results were news stories that were "light, careless, ephemeral, intended to entertain or instruct for a day and then sink into oblivion" while a well-written magazine article had polish, permanence, and "something of the air and dignity of a book about it."[15] However, the similarities between fiction and news and the fact that some successful journalists were also successful short-story and novel writers indicated that the two narrative forms shared at least a few rungs on the same career ladders.

The definitions of news that late-nineteenth-century editors and reporters debated differed from the one offered at mid-century by Horace Greeley, editor of the *New York Tribune*. Greeley was an influential journalist. He had trained Charles A. Dana, later editor of the *New York Sun*, and H. J. Raymond, editor of the *New York Times*. His *Tribune* was considered one of the most important newspapers published in the United States.[16] He urged his correspondents to produce stories about "facts, incidents, occurrences, at the earliest moment."[17] The facts in the story should be "stronger" than the words used to discuss them. Greeley, however, made two points that late-nineteenth-century editors and reporters might disagree with. Greeley's news was categorical and inanimate: He wanted facts, incidents, and occurrences. The 1890s reporter or editor would add that the people controlling the facts and events were equally as important. Greeley and other editors of the period also accepted the notion that correspondents might express opinion in their stories.[18] By the end of the century, the same practice would be questionable.

Avoiding opinion was the first of five rules of reporting that Baker, a veteran of the *Chicago Record*, included in his autobiography.[19] Kent Cooper, who reported for several Indiana newspapers before joining the Associated Press management team, recorded a similar rule in his work memoir: "I could write facts. I could not express my own opinions."[20] Instead, it was the reporter's job to hunt for the news "which means the interesting, the unusual, surprising, shocking, remarkable, wonderful, wicked, horrible—not the commonplace, the expected, the normal" things that people do.[21] The news also could be what another journalist failed to report.[22] The value of a piece of news depended upon the number of people interested in it, according to a contributor to *The Journalist*.[23] That value could be expressed in geographic terms—rain in Arizona would be news, but not in New Orleans.[24] What normally was not news might be elevated to that status on slow news days.[25] Events and people generally lost their news value with time. "Remember always that to-day's news is twice as good as yesterday's, news two days old or more is ordinarily well-nigh useless," wrote John Palmer Gavit, a contributor to *The Journalist*.[26] The interconnections among event or subject, audience, and reporter were captured in a collection of speeches and essays by James Luby, a former *New York Sun* editor. Luby, who had been drafting a journalism textbook at the time of his death, wrote that news was anything interesting to intelligent men or women that had not been reported before. The energy and expense a newspaper expended to acquire a story were related to the audience's interest in it. Luby wrote:

> But whether the news be great or small, the principles and methods of obtaining it are always the same. To the place where the news has developed or is expected to develop a man or a woman is sent to gather the facts and form a clear comprehension of them. A small man is sent after small news; a skilled man upon greater occasions; the masters of the craft are mobilized in wartime.[27]

Defining news seemed difficult for Gilded Age journalists, but from their perspective, little doubt existed about why the demand for news continued to grow. The social and political environments were changing; the industrial revolution had provided journalism with the machines needed to quickly publish large newspapers, and the war had turned Americans into readers.[28] A contributor to the *Chautauquan* observed that almost overnight the industry's standard four-page newspaper had doubled in size; the semi-weekly had evolved into a daily; transmission of news by telegraph had increased a hundredfold, and new, fast presses had been invented to spread news "before the eyes of millions of eager, devouring readers."[29] E. L. Shuman, author of *Steps into Journalism*, the popular guidebook for those considering careers in journalism, estimated that the aggregate circulation of newspapers in the 1880s was two billion, or about forty copies for each man, woman, and child. Half a dozen newspapers with daily circulations of more than 100,000 and several others with double that volume existed.[30] At mid-century, however, all the New York dailies combined did not print more than 10,000 copies a day. Greeley, for instance, printed 5,000 copies of the *New York Tribune*'s first edition. Subscribers bought a tenth of the press run; newsboys gave most of the remainder away.[31]

Rather than seek a shared definition, some Gilded Age reporters, editors, and publishers believed it easier to say what news was not. One such definition noted that: "News is not gossip, nor romance, nor history, nor literature, nor opinion."[32] Sunday metropolitan newspapers had become so large by the 1890s that some suggested that news be treated as a commodity, rather than a concept, and be sold by the pound.[33] The result was a collage: Some definitions were fanciful. Irvin Cobb, for instance, called the results of reporting an "inky-nosed, nine-eyed, clay-footed god called News."[34] Other definitions were scholarly; a few, economic and geographic. Others tried to constrict the flow of news instead of defining it. Editors at the *Chicago Tribune* provided rural correspondents with a list of nineteen categories of events and people not to be treated as news. Items that were based on rumors or that were "puff" pieces promoting businesses should not be considered news. Fatalities or accidents involving railroad employees or obscure people were not to be used except "when two or more fatalities result from the same accident or there is a great loss of property involved."[35] Likewise, obituaries for ordinary citizens should not be written, but death notices about prominent state or national figures should be provided.

Academics matched journalism's struggle with its key concept by struggling to produce a concrete definition of literature. One wrote that it was not possible to say literature was any particular thing because its subject matter could be anything. The only safe course identified literature as not the same as narratives that only conveyed information.[36] H. W. Crawshaw, professor of English literature at Colgate University, agreed with that dichotomy but little else. "Definitions of literature are legion; and most current conceptions of it are vague and ambiguous," he wrote.[37] Crawshaw broadly defined literature as art. Harvard University English professor Adams Sherman Hill believed journalism could never, in any of its forms, take the place of literature. He wrote: "It does not, as literature does, lift us out of the trivial interests and petty passions of daily life into a pure and invigorating air."[38]

Successfully drawing a distinction hardly mattered in a theatre-going and book-reading country like the United States. Ill-prepared newspaper reviewers set the standard that literary excellence did not matter, but popularity did, wrote a *New York Commercial Advertiser*'s drama critic.[39]

Hill saw little difference between the quality of writing in second-class novels and in newspapers. Both were ephemeral; both used what Hill and others referred to as "newspaper English." Both contained grammatical errors, used cliché constructions, created neologisms, or turned nouns into verbs.[40] A contributor to the *Fourth Estate* agreed with many of Hill's conclusions: "[T]he two professions are so closely linked as to make it difficult to know where one ends and the other begins. True, all journalism is not literature, but the foundation of the latter is so firmly grounded in the former as to make journalism an integral part of the whole structure."[41] Sometimes, both novelists and reporters usurped what they imagined to be the diction and syntax of the upper social classes: "'Scribes of this class, as they call themselves, 'savor' their wine instead of tasting it . . ."[42] Novelists read newspapers, and reporters read shoddy novels, thus cross-contaminating each other. The real battle among critics, professors, and journalists was over the rapid spread of "newspaper English." Academics blamed novice reporters for its spread. To meet the "enormous" Gilded Age demand for reporters, ill-prepared writers had been admitted into journalism.[43] Their flawed output exceeded the ability of editors to correct their work.

Journalists saw it differently. After years of editing news stories generated by recent college graduates, Archie Emerson Palmer concluded that the faculties at Harvard, Princeton, Yale, and Cornell had demonstrated they could not teach syntax and diction to their students.[44] If he had to rank institutions' ability to do so, Palmer would place Princeton first for teaching good grammar. Graduates who could write adequate English were "a rare exception; and as for punctuation—a matter almost as important as correct spelling and unimpeachable grammar,—not one man in a hundred knew the proper use of a single punctuation mark except the period," he added.[45] Practical guides to newspaper English generated by editors and publishers like Shuman, Robert Luce, and some of the serial contributors to trade journals would continue to be needed in journalism.

Others were less pessimistic. A contributor to the *Austin Daily Statesman* argued that plain English was the quickest way to reach the largest audience. Newspapers had been condemned by academics for "using colloquialisms, vulgarisms if you please . . . but what the newspaper tries to do is make itself intelligible to the largest number of people in the shortest time and smallest space."[46] The *Fourth Estate* contributor wrote that it was unfair to criticize the grammar used in newspapers because newspapers were the product of one day's effort while a book could take several years to produce. Franklin Matthews, a *Philadelphia Press* editor who would become an associate professor in the new Pulitzer-funded Columbia School of Journalism, ranked newspaper English as worse than the English used from the pulpit and in literature, but better than the English used in the business world, and superior to that heard in ordinary conversations.[47] Journalism's priority was to publish before deadline rather than use superior English. He cited three reasons why grammar errors persisted in newspapers: 1) Publishers hired cheap labor. These workers were likely to use slang, clumsy phrases, and stock expressions; 2) Readers, especially in smaller markets, liked home-spun writing; and 3) Haste in publishing, especially in larger markets, permitted some errors to slip by.

There had been some progress. Journalism had refined diction and syntax rules to clarify meaning and to condense stories by eliminating non-essential words and clichés. Gavit estimated that a reporter using those refinements could cut the length of his or her stories by 20 percent.[48] Articles and books like Gavit's and Shuman's were spreading those space-saving tricks throughout newspaperdom. Those sources agreed that newspaper English should exclude qualifying adverbs and adjectives, use the appropriate verb tenses, eliminate slang, and respect the rules for forming degrees of comparison. Some words already represented "the maximum of force—100 percent words, so to speak," according to Alex G. Nevins, who wrote a two-part series on copy-editing for *The Journalist*.[49] Those words—like *destroyed*, *devoted*, *false*, and *solved*—did not require additional words like *completely* to express clear meaning. Other qualifying words that could be eliminated from newspaper English included *awful*, *ghastly*, *horrible*, *terrible*, *sickening*, and *appalling*. "Forms of expression" also could be condensed by eliminating extraneous words like *with* from *consult with*, *met with*, and others.[50] Honorary or courtesy titles should be used sparingly.[51] In an exchange between a fictional reporter and a young man considering a journalism career, *Outlook* satirized some examples of popular clichés that could be eliminated: "When a gentleman gives a bank-note it must always be a 'crisp' five-dollar or ten-dollar one," and "Thuds are of two descriptions, the 'dull' and the 'sickening.'"[52]

These sources offered other refinements that protected the value of news by using the appropriate language. Luce, author of *Writing for the Press: A Manual for Editors, Reporters, Correspondents, and Printers*, cautioned new reporters to be careful how they used the phrases "the other day," "not long ago," and "recently." Those constructions indicated an item too old to have value as news.[53] Young reporters also should learn how to write "for" and "against" space. Writing for space meant the common practice of writing a specified number of words, but a new reporter also could learn from that experience how to spin or pad a story "without making it dull."[54]

Mastering these skills helped both the aspiring reporter and aspiring novelist to put a foot on the first rung of the ladder of the literary career described by multiple nineteenth-century authors.[55] Obtaining a position as a reporter was the next rung.[56] Assuming that applicants came from small towns or a rural environment, Shuman shared this advice: "Journalism, like charity and missionary work, should if possible begin at home."[57] To continue to climb the ladder, the novice should get a job on a local daily or weekly newspaper by submitting unsolicited articles to the editors. The first story should be: "A brief and well written communication on some topic of interest—not yourself or your family affairs—but a bright, attractive half-column sketch . . ."[58] After a few of those stories were published and the writer had learned to incorporate in later items the editor's corrections, the novice should apply for a full-time position. Following more experience, the novice could branch out by also serving as a metropolitan daily's correspondent. The process could be repeated until the reporter secured a chance to "try-out" for a large daily's staff.[59] The established metropolitan reporter could then venture into fiction and non-fiction writing for magazines. Those with sufficient talent might write novels for either the adult or juvenile markets or plays for the theatre. Some—like Richard Harding Davis and Elizabeth L. Banks—could spend a sizable portion of their careers as freelancers working in both fiction and non-fiction. The results could be lucrative. Davis and Rudyard Kipling, for instance, reportedly earned twenty-five cents a word on some commissions from editors.[60] By comparison, the *Brooklyn Eagle* paid five dollars per 1,200- to 1,400-word column.

Some skills mastered by journalists as they moved up the occupational ladder were interchangeable with literary work. Kirk Munroe dedicated his novel, *Under Orders: The Story of a Young Reporter*, to *New York Sun* city editor John Bogart. Munroe credited Bogart with helping him to develop a literary style in his news writing.[61] Munroe eventually wrote thirty-five novels, mostly for boys, and was the first editor of *Harper's Round Table*. James Lauren Ford's stint at the *New York Herald* and other newspapers provided him with the basis for characters that populated his newspaper satires published in *Life*, *Cosmopolitan*, and *Puck*. Augustus Thomas, the playwright, recommended working on a metropolitan newspaper as one of three methods to prepare for a career in the theatre. The other two were the study of good plays and a period of professional acting. Working at a newspaper was valuable because "the reporter learns news values, and the climactic situation for a play would be almost always a first-page story in a newspaper office," Thomas wrote.[62] Working at the *St. Louis Post-Dispatch* also had taught him the similarities between the interview and character dialogue as well as how to "draw" a subject for the stage. One of Thomas's plays, *A Man of the World*, was a reworked newspaper story that *Post-Dispatch* editors had rejected. In one year, *A Man of the World* earned Thomas $3,000 in royalties, an example, he said, of the difference in pecuniary rewards for the two professions. If asked to pick between the royalties and the training he had received on newspapers, however, Thomas said he would take the latter.

Climbing the literary ladder through newspapers, magazines, short stories, and novels looked attractive, but it might not always be lucrative. Those who attempted to start the climb as a freelancer did not earn much at first. After surveying the policies of daily newspapers, weeklies, and monthly magazines in the New York City market, a writer for *The Independent* concluded that a beginner with good story ideas and a willingness to work hard might earn from $750 to $1,000, about the same as an established reporter with a salary of fifteen or twenty dollars a week. To do so without an agent, the writer would have to contend with long delays about publication decisions, equally long delays in receiving payment, manuscript readers who judged the merits of a piece on the basis of the contributor's handwriting, and unscrupulous editors who rejected work but pirated the story ideas. The beginner survived in spite of the editors rather than because of them. To further complicate matters, the professional writer could expect competition from multiple, nonprofessional sources. The *Independent* contributor, using the pen name "Every Day Scribbler," wrote that the "trades of author and newspaper man are hopelessly mixed. Tempted by a fat fee and a large audience, your historian, essay writer, scientist, yes, and clergyman, will turn his hand to an editorial in a Sunday paper, and allow his portrait and signature to be printed along with it, and by the same token, your literary man has, in three cases out of four, been a reporter for the daily press."[63]

In the American book market, publishers also had the upper hand in negotiating contracts with authors, novelist W. D. Howells found.[64] Book deals, for instance, ranged from those in which the author paid all the expenses of publication, and the publisher received a percentage of the book's retail price for managing the project, to publishers offering the author 10 percent of the book's retail price after the first thousand copies sold. Marketing efforts, according to Howells, did not seem to improve book sales: "Advertising will not avail, and reviewing is notoriously futile."[65] What did matter, especially in the case of fiction, was the reaction of women readers, who drove the American market for books.

Known authors could increase their incomes by serializing their work in magazines, which were prospering, Howells wrote. Those who produced non-fiction like interviews with important people, popular science stories, and travelogues should target newspaper syndicates, whose clients were the Sunday editions of newspapers with their "vast demand" for material to fill twelve-, eighteen-, twenty-four-, and thirty-six-page editions.[66]

Literary agents working independently of publishing houses to place authors' works appeared both in the United States and Britain during the final decades of the nineteenth century and offered authors some relief. These "cultural managers," as Charles Johanningsmeier and others referred to them, aided authors to efficiently route content to print outlets, to interpret complex publishing contracts, and to understand and exploit new, international copyright laws.[67] A good agent did more than just place an author's work. Some provided proofreading services, demanded advances and higher royalties for their clients, and ensured payment on publication.

Journalism's conflict with literature over the definition of key concepts signaled a jurisdiction dispute between occupations. This dispute matched the newsroom CoP, where reporters and editors served as knowledge brokers, with the classroom and literary market CoP, where English professors, reviewers, and book publishers performed the knowledge broker tasks. Similarities between literature and news complicated this work. The novices guided by these knowledge brokers shared some rungs on the same career ladder; they shared some of the same, basic academic training; they often structured narrative and dialogue in the same manner. Differences also existed. Literary work was marketed differently than news paid for on the space system, and "newspaper English" could be blamed either on university faculties or bad habits learned in the newsroom. Journalism's ability to create and maintain distinct occupational boundaries and to train the new labor force depended upon what "life competencies" knowledge brokers successfully transmitted to their students. Their stature as accomplished and authoritative practitioners would help determine their success.

Chapter Four

# The Rule Writers

Novices learned some of the "life competencies" of newswork by trial and error, but senior news professionals acting as knowledge brokers also helped by producing non-fiction and fiction artifacts. Their fiction output was so voluminous that short stories and novels are analyzed in a later chapter. Unplanned interactions between the novice and the knowledge broker also played a role. The curriculum shared through books, magazines, the trade press, and face-to-face exchanges ranged from lessons in press nomenclature to basic grammar, the work environment a novice likely would encounter, and the preparatory steps he or she should take before embarking on a journalism career.

Many narratives began by discouraging job hopefuls. A contributor to the *Journalist* wrote: "The first rule, therefore, to be followed in writing for the press is, Don't. The second is Don't any more than you can possibly help; and the third is, if you must do it, get discouraged as soon as possible. Any person who will carefully follow these three rules cannot fail to make a success of literary work."[1] A writer for another trade publication called newswork "the profession of last resort."[2]

Judging how influential these non-fiction narratives were is difficult. The journalists examined here seldom mentioned their reading habits, but circulation numbers are available for some periodicals that frequently discussed the news profession. For instance, *Lippincott's Magazine*, the *Chautauquan*, and *Forum* frequently published articles explaining the conventions of journalism and the inner workings of city rooms. *Lippincott's*, which did not release circulation numbers, published a fourteen-part *Journalist Series* between January 1892 and December 1893. Most contributors to the series were journalists. Media historian Frank Luther

Mott estimated *Forum*'s circulation at 20,000 in 1888, but that number declined through the remainder of the century.[3] *The Chautauquan* was published by the Chautauqua Literary and Scientific Circle, an adult education project popular in the nineteenth century. It estimated in 1885 that the magazine's circulation was 50,000.[4] Of three New York-based trade journals published in the late nineteenth century that focused on newswork, *The Journalist* offered more information for the rank-and-file newsroom employee; some of its content has been examined in previous chapters.[5] *The Journalist*'s self-reported circulation reached 7,500 in 1888, but it often reproduced in pamphlet form instructive serials which it then sold for a dime.[6] Reliable sales numbers for these spin-off publications are not available.

Guide or "how-to-do-it" books had varying levels of success. Three of the more important are examined here: E. L. Shuman's *Steps Into Journalism: Helps and Hints for Young Writers*; Robert Luce's *Writing for the Press: A Manual for Editors, Reporters, Correspondents, and Printers*; and Martha L. Rayne's *What Can a Woman Do: Her Position in the Business and Literary World*. Rayne's volume was first published in 1884, but eight other reprints and revised editions were issued between then and 1896. Luce's book appeared in five editions between 1886 and 1907. Shuman's *Steps Into Journalism* appeared in a single 1894 edition, but Shuman followed it with *Practical Journalism*, a sequel for experienced reporters. Other, smaller publications existed, but they did not appear to have the same appeal for readers. For instance, the Chicago Society of Proof Readers published a sixteen-page style book that could be purchased in pamphlet format; its goal was to help proofreaders and printers establish a uniform style at local newspapers and job printing offices.

Future reporter and magazine editor H. L. Mencken found Shuman's book helpful in the early stages of his career.[7] Shuman wrote *Steps Into Journalism* during his first job as a reporter and editor at the *Chicago Journal*, a position that he secured partly through family connections. Shuman paid many of his college expenses by working part-time as a printer's devil, compositor, proofreader, reporter, and editor. A graduate of Northwestern University, he organized the first student press on that campus. It eventually became the commercial Evanston Press. *Steps Into Journalism* focused on the technicalities of newswork, explaining the hierarchy of workers within a newsroom and the basic errors that a beginner might make and their solutions. An earlier version of his book was used as a text for a course offered through the Chautauquan Assembly at Bay View, Michigan.

Luce's book focused more on proofreading and typography, but he also offered advice for the beginning reporter. A Harvard graduate, Luce worked as a *Boston Globe* reporter from 1884 to 1888. He and a brother then established the Luce Press Clipping Bureau in New York. Luce also represented Massachusetts for twenty years in multiple state and federal elective offices.

Rayne's *What Can a Woman Do* sold more than 100,000 copies.[8] Women professionals cited it as a source of inspiration more than seventy years after its initial publication.[9] Rayne was editor and publisher of the *Chicago Magazine of Fashion, Music and Home Reading* from 1870 to 1876, a Sunday writer for the *Chicago Tribune*, a staff member at the *Detroit Free Press*, and correspondent for several other newspapers. Historians sometimes credit her with establishing the first proprietary school of journalism in 1886 in Detroit.[10] Her book explored career possibilities for women in law, medicine, music, and several other professions. Rayne devoted separate chapters to literature and to journalism. The journalism chapter investigated a number of strategies job seekers could use to obtain their first job and to succeed in subsequent positions. The advice included preliminary instruction about writing basic stories.

The texts, like Shuman's that were meant strictly for those considering a career in journalism, offered readers a finer-grained discussion of news-related topics: Hierarchies within newsrooms, the nomenclature commonly used by journalists, successful story structures, and routine sources. These texts also acknowledged that journalism encompassed idiosyncratic and unarticulated conventions as well.

More general-interest publications like *Lippincott's* series offered readers the knowledge "common" to journalism and served the same function that introductory textbooks performed in other occupations. These conventions represented what Irvin Cobb called the "mechanical" or "academic" rules of journalism. A beginner learned "them so that customarily he knows how to obey them, and also he learns those rules so that intelligently he may know when and where to break them,"[11] Cobb wrote. He offered an example from his own career: He had abandoned the inverted pyramid story format when writing about a hydrophobia victim. He began the story in the middle with a lead paragraph that said the man had three days to live.

Much of the nomenclature of the late nineteenth century and discussed in these texts would endure into the twentieth century.[12] Others required translation from one region to the next. Boston news men referred to "exclusives" while New York reporters used the terms "beat" or "scoop" to signify the same type of story that one newspaper, not others, had.[13] No matter the label, both terms referred to the "highest aim and the proudest achievement" that a news person could score.[14] A "beat" also could refer to specific institutions or topics that a reporter was assigned to cover. A reporter who had acquired the most scoops in a newsroom was that newspaper's "star" or "leading" reporter.[15] Women attempting to break into newswork sometimes wrote "specials" or "Sunday specials." Specials were long articles treating in detail one or all of the three types of content which a newspaper used—news, editorials, and general reading matter.[16] The "city room" was the same as the "local room," the place where the city editor and reporters had their desks.[17] A "cub" generally meant a reporter in the first year of newswork, but it could be longer.[18] It did not mean a novice trying out for a reporting job. Cubs had been or expected to be hired; those doing try-outs had not. Reporters who were paid on "space," or by how much of what they wrote was published, submitted a weekly "string." These reporters cut their published stories out of the newspaper and pasted them together. The "string" was measured and the reporter paid for the number of columns the string represented.[19] Some newspapers paid additional sums to "long-watch" men who stayed in the newsroom of morning newspapers until 4:00 a.m. or to space reporters who waited in the newsroom, but received no assignment. Beginning reporters usually were assigned to the "long watch."

Ideal candidates for an apprentice reporter's position prepared early by reading great works of literature and by developing precision in written communication that employed a vocabulary "accessible to common people."[20] Exposure to a university curriculum emphasizing literature, economics, politics, and related subjects was helpful. Course work that taught some of the rudimentary skills of journalism might reduce the length of a cub's apprenticeship.[21] Allan Forman of *The Journalist* believed that instruction that included work on a collegiate publication would not only benefit a cub reporter, but improve journalism's image and inject some standardization into the field, which he believed had little. Journalism as yet had no fixed doctrine that could be easily taught.[22] Forman and others agreed that a liberal arts education alone was insufficient preparation for newswork. Journalism required what Joseph Pulitzer and others called "intuitive skills" that could be refined only through supervised observation and practice, the same route taken by a new doctor or lawyer.[23] Developing a "nose for news," learning how to read human nature, and perfecting the ability to pursue a difficult investigation were among those skills.

Candidates also should be willing to start on a country or small-town newspaper where they could be exposed to all aspects of journalism and could develop Pulitzer's intuitive skills.[24] Once hired, new reporters were expected to handle massive workloads. Ray Stannard Baker, for instance, wrote 3,000 to 4,000 words each eleven-hour work day at the *Chicago Record*.[25] As managing editor of a Detroit newspaper, Charles Edward Russell expected his reporters to produce 1,000 longhand words per hour.[26] Florence Finch Kelly generated more than eight columns a week by longhand at the *Boston Globe*.[27] She also substituted for the literary editor and sometimes critiqued theatre productions. Elizabeth Jordan worked fourteen- to eighteen-hour days at the *New York World*.[28]

Besides intelligence, good health, and youth, the cub needed courage and coolness to master some assignments.[29] Honorable behavior and a willingness to work also were needed. In short, the young reporter should reflect the virtues of his fellow citizens, wrote William Henry Smith, an Associated Press manager. "The American is vigorous, active, and dexterous, and the journalist preeminently represents the national character," he told readers of *Century Magazine*.[30]

Cubs also had to learn two hierarchies: One for editors and a second for reporters. Editors had feudal-like authority over reporters.[31] On very large metropolitan newspapers, the managing editor was responsible for the news content. Reporting to him was the city editor (often responsible for news within a hundred-mile radius) and the telegraph editor (responsible for collecting correspondent and news association coverage of the rest of the world). There were department editors for specialized news like real estate, business, railroads, and book and theatre reviews. Often overlooked in the discussion of this editing hierarchy was the night editor at morning newspapers.[32] The night editor was responsible for covering any late, non-routine news. Finally, most newspapers had an "exchange" editor who read other newspapers and clipped stories that might be of use to his publication. A new reporter with some experience could be assigned to the "exchange" editorship.[33]

Besides the distinction between cubs and more experienced reporters, reporters could be sorted into several additional categories. A "general" assignment reporter had no set beat and covered a range of events and people.[34] Experienced reporters could be further divided between reporters who covered local events and "special correspondents" who were dispatched to cover far away stories like wars, trials involving prominent citizens, or news from Washington, D.C., or from statehouses.

There were no regional differences when knowledge brokers shared advice about story structure. Shuman offered this common summary: "Begin with the most striking fact in the whole story. Make the first two or three sentences tell the whole in a nutshell. Then begin a new paragraph and start in on the details, enlarging on the subject as much as necessary to fill the limit of words allowed you."[35] Other knowledge brokers offered amplification. In a three-part series printed in a trade journal, Alex G. Nevins of the *New York Morning Journal* advised new reporters: "If prominent people are involved, use their names early; if the circumstances are more important, mention them first."[36] Deadlines were to be observed. Good grammar was encouraged. Names should be spelled correctly and middle initials used if possible. Stories that transmitted the most ideas in the fewest words were valued.[37] Knowledge brokers reminded reporters to reproduce facts and the opinions of sources, not their own. Routine sources—undertakers, bartenders, livery stable owners, barbers, health officials, police officers, hotel clerks, and others—should be cultivated.

While text-based artifacts like these had the potential to efficiently knit together many CoPs into a constellation of practitioners who shared the same basic knowledge, autobiographers recalled learning and teaching in other ways.[38] An equally important conduit appeared to be webs of professional relationships not always confined to the cub's city room. A variety of knowledge brokers shared these webs, and they could guide cub reporters through this complex geography of hierarchies, rules, techniques, and routines. To be effective guides, knowledge brokers had to be perceived as accomplished workers who shared innovations by example or through generating durable and informative work artifacts. They could perform those roles in any of three "broker" categories: boundary spanners who maintained barriers between their CoP and others, roamers who moved knowledge from place to place, and outposts who explored new areas and brought back news from them to their own CoP.

Innovations and work standards circulated through four types of relationships among cubs and knowledge brokers.[39] Those connections included: 1) interactions between cub reporters and their city editors or star reporters, 2) interactions with reporters from competing newspapers, 3) interactions with the editors of other types of periodicals who purchased freelance work from beginners, and 4) interactions through social groups. Thus, some cub reporters could be simultaneously socialized to newswork through overlapping networks of knowledge brokers. The peripatetic nature of nineteenth-century newswork ensured that these knowledge brokers would circulate through a variety of newsrooms. Firings were common and competition for jobs fierce.[40] As knowledge brokers moved from job to job, they shared innovations they had learned elsewhere.

The *New York Sun* provides a good example of how this dynamic worked. Its editors were known for training cubs and for producing more journeymen reporters than any other New York City newspaper, according to one contemporary observer.[41] The *Sun's* editor for much of this period, Charles Anderson Dana, was considered by many to be the profession's leader.[42] *Sun* editors also had earned a reputation for introducing journalistic innovations. They honed the interview, originally introduced to American journalism by the elder James Gordon Bennett, editor of the *New York Herald*, as a means for routinely acquiring information.[43] *Sun* reporters and editors also experimented with story structure—deleting "the weary introductions that had been the fashion in newspapers—leading paragraphs which told over again what was in the head-lines and were merely a prelude to a third and detailed telling."[44] Into this new structure reporters learned to pour "tight," concisely written stories.[45] *Sun* editors also prized originality in writing. "Clarity, vividness, and interest" generally were required of any story appearing in its pages.[46]

The *Sun* also was a pioneer in refining a fresh category of news, the human interest story. Apocryphal or not, *Sun* city editor John B. Bogart was credited with the "man bites dog" exemplum of human interest. Amos Jay Cummings, one of the *Sun's* early managing editors until he found his niche as a reporter, was known in newspaper circles as one of the first real human-interest reporters. One of Cummings's colleagues said the *Sun* editor understood the news value of the "steer loose in the streets, the lost child in the police station, the Italian murder that was really a case of vendetta."[47] Julius Chambers, who had worked for New York dailies beginning with the *New York Tribune* staff under Greeley in 1870 and ending as managing editor of the *New York World* in 1889, offered this example of a story possessing universal appeal for readers because of human interest:

> Imagine, for example, a murder at midnight, in the fashionable part of a great city! A distinguished banker has been assassinated in his bedroom. The crime will become the universal theme of conversation and wonder on the following day. So fierce is the rivalry between the morning journals that all want complete accounts of the terrible event.[48]

Tapping the "vital quality" found in human interest stories would become a standard for news writing by at least 1884, according to John W. Perry, who compared New York dailies published in 1884 and 1934.[49] If news was defined as what type of story appeared on page one, then little had changed in fifty years. Perry wrote that the 1884 reader "could learn the latest big news, which most generally had to do with politics, and he could chuckle over local gossip and be regaled with long stories by popular novelists of the time, just as present-day newspaper readers do. Stories that generally made Page One in 1884 would make Page One in 1934."[50]

Twenty-three of the fifty-five journalists examined in this book were selected for additional study because their careers illustrated how knowledge brokers evolved (see table opposite). The twenty-three were drawn from a list of former *Sun* reporters and editors. Their work histories were reconstructed in whole or in part from biographical dictionaries, obituaries, and other sources.[51] All had entered the *Sun* newsroom as novices or partly trained cubs, were exposed to the *Sun*'s news innovations including the human interest story, and emerged as knowledge brokers.

*New York Sun* "Alumni" and Their Careers

| Name | Birth year | News job before the *Sun* (full-time) | Dates at the *Sun* | Last news job |
|---|---|---|---|---|
| Adams, Samuel Hopkins | 1871 | None, *New York Sun* is first | 1891–1900 | *McClure's*, novelist |
| Block, Rudolph Edgar (Bruno Lessing) | 1870 | None, *New York Sun* is first | 1888–1894 | Editor, Hearst comic supplement |
| Brisbane, Arthur | 1864 | None, *New York Sun* is first | 1883–1890 | Newspaper proprietor, Hearst syndicated columnist |
| Denison, Lindsay | 1873 | Assistant editor, *Cosmopolitan Magazine* | 1896–1904 | *New York World* special writer |
| Fairbanks, Charles Mason | 1855 | *Cleveland Herald* | Unknown | Art correspondent, *New York Times* |
| Ford, James Lauren | 1854 | *Railroad Gazette* | Unknown | Editor, *The Porcupine*, author |
| Forman, Henry James | 1879 | None, *New York Sun* is first | 1903–1914 | Editor, *Collier's*, author |
| Irwin, William Henry | 1873 | Sunday editor, *San Francisco Chronicle* | 1903–1906 | Contributor, *Collier's*, author |
| Kobbe, Gustav | 1857 | Editor, *Musical Review* | 1881–1882 | *New York Herald* |
| Mackenzie, Cameron | 1882 | None, *New York Sun* is first | 1901–1906 | *McClure's*, author |
| Matthews, (Albert) Franklin | 1858 | *New York World* | 1890–1909 | Faculty member, Pulitzer School of Journalism |
| Moody, Helen Watterson | 1860 | *Cleveland Leader* | 1887–1891 | Editor, McClure's Syndicate |
| Mott, Edward Harold | 1845 | Editor, *Milford (Penn.) Herald* | Unknown | Editor, *Goshen (N.Y.) Independent Republican* |
| Munroe, Kirk | 1850 | None, *New York Sun* is first | Unknown | Author, juvenile fiction; editor, *Harper's Young People* |
| O'Brien, Frank Michael | 1875 | *Buffalo Courier* | 1904–1905 | Editor, *New York Sun* |
| Oulahan, Richard V. | 1867 | Washington Bureau, United Press | 1897–1912 | Correspondent, *New York Times* |
| Ritchie, Robert Welles | 1879 | *San Francisco Call-Bulletin* | 1906–1913 | Hearst London Bureau |
| Rosebault, Charles J. | 1865 | Unknown | 1884–1907 | Business manager, *New York Sun* |
| Selden, Charles Albert | 1870 | *Providence Journal* | 1900–1904 | Correspondent, *New York Times* |
| Simonds, Frank Herbert | 1878 | *New York Evening Post* | 1908–1914 | *Review of Reviews* |
| Van Anda, Carr V. | 1864 | Night editor, *Baltimore Sun* | 1888–1904 | Managing editor, *New York Times* |
| Whiting, Robert Rudd | 1877 | None, *New York Sun* is first | 1899–1904 | Editor, writer, *Ainslee's* |
| Williams, Talcott | 1849 | Washington correspondent, *New York World* | 1877–1879 | Director, Pulitzer School of Journalism |

Reference works disagree about some of the dates and work assignments listed in the table above. In those cases, the dates and work locations cited by most sources are used.

Fifteen of the alumni had had previous reporting or editing experience before they joined the *Sun*. For the most part, that experience had been on smaller metropolitan newspapers like the *Cleveland Herald* or *Buffalo Courier* or on specialty publications like the New York-based *Railroad Gazette*. Most had not held substantial reporting and editing positions before joining the *Sun*. For seven, like Arthur Brisbane, working at the *Sun* appeared to be their first, full-time, paid job in journalism. More than half were in their twenties or younger when *Sun* editors hired them. Included on the list are Carr V. Van Anda, who would become managing editor of the *New York Times;* future muckrakers Samuel Hopkins Adams and Will Irwin; Talcott Williams, the first director of Columbia University's Pulitzer-funded School of Journalism, and Franklin Matthews, an associate professor at the school who had worked with Williams at the *Philadelphia Press*.

Most joined the *Sun* staff in the last quarter of the nineteenth century and stayed an average of eight years. Twenty of the twenty-three held seventy-one news-related jobs, an average of 3.55 positions per alumnus, after their work on the *Sun*. After leaving the *Sun*, most functioned as "roamers" or "outposts." Brisbane is a good example of a "roamer." In his seven years at the *Sun*, he worked as a reporter, London correspondent, and editor. For the next seven years, he worked as managing editor of the *New York World*. Finally, William Randolph Hearst recruited Brisbane to edit the *New York Evening Journal*. After that, Brisbane bought, edited, or sold newspaper properties for Hearst and wrote a weekly syndicated column. Frank M. O'Brien and Charles Mason Fairbanks more closely fit the description of "outposts." O'Brien worked for the *Sun* between 1904 and 1905 and then again from 1916 to 1918. He returned to the *Sun* in 1924 as an editorial writer after having worked for the *New York Herald*. He finished his career as editor of the newspaper from 1926 to 1943. During his absences, O'Brien worked as editorial and special writer for the *New York Press* and the *New York Herald*. Fairbanks also had an on-again, off-again connection with the *Sun*. He quit the *New York World* to join the *Sun*, then left to be night editor of the *Baltimore Sun*. He then joined the *Cleveland Argus*, one of his father's publishing ventures. Eventually, he returned to the *Sun* and worked as a reporter and in other editorial positions. He left once more to join an advertising agency.

Some of the twenty-three produced text-based artifacts after leaving the *Sun* that could be instructive for cubs. These items included both fiction and non-fiction books, magazine articles, short stories, and work autobiographies. Examples included Adams's four newspaper-related novels and a textbook written by Williams. The artifacts produced by the *Sun* group as well as other memoir writers shared some common themes. In general, the authors explained what they learned about newswork and how they learned it during their first years in journalism. They frequently imparted lessons about finding, cultivating, and interviewing sources. Some explained how to avoid trouble with a particular newspaper's "sacred cows." This final category was more about what not to write than it was about what should be written.

The physical layout of most nineteenth-century newspaper offices could give cub reporters an advantage in the learning process: proximity to editors and star reporters. Everyone involved in the news-gathering effort, be it local, regional, or national, usually occupied offices on the same floor of a newspaper.[52] Samuel Blythe, who compared reporters to society's scouts, explained in his autobiography that it was essential that every man on the newspaper should be in close communication with these "scouts." He called them the mainspring of the paper. A cub reporter's first destination on this floor likely was the city (or news) room, described as the "barracks of the reportorial corps," the place where the beginner was likely to have his or her first introduction to the journalistic world."[53] The key knowledge broker in this room was the city editor, who managed reporters covering local news. He decided what stories a beginner could attempt, judged their progress or lack of it, and taught cubs the literal, relative value of news stories by explaining how many column inches a story should consume.[54]

How physical proximity in the city room helped the cub learn the rudiments of newswork depended in part upon the temperament of the city editor and, in some cases, that of experienced reporters. Mencken was fortunate to report to the rare city editor who explained newswork to him and patiently edited his stories while Mencken looked on.

Mencken wrote in his memoir that the city editor taught him:

> *Imprimis*, never trust a cop: whenever possible, verify his report. *Item*, always try to get in early copy: the first story to reach the city-desk has a

> much better chance of being printed in full than the last. *Item*, be careful about dates, names, ages, addresses, figures of every sort. *Item*, keep in mind at all times the dangers of libel. Finally, don't be surprised if you go to a house for information, and are invited to lift it from the *Sun* of the next morning. The *Sun* is the Bible of Baltimore, and has almost a monopoly on many kinds of news. But don't let that fact discourage you.[55]

The instruction that Mencken received found parallels in many other city rooms, but the delivery could be different. Isaac Marcosson recalled that *Louisville Times* city editor John A. Baird "slashed the life out of my early 'copy,' but there was a lesson in every scratch of his pencil."[56] Augustus Thomas had the good fortune to occupy a desk adjacent to *St. Louis Post-Dispatch* city editor John Magner, giving him an opportunity to hear Magner tutor other reporters. The city editor of a Chicago newspaper used the same direct approach to teach Kelly. Sent to cover a story at a rail station about a shipment of "white slaves," she missed the train, but managed to get a story from railroad employees. Kelly's outrage over the treatment of the women showed in her story. The city editor "blue-penciled my copy a little, telling me kindly that I must not put editorial or personal comments into a news article or report, but must make it a straight, impartial account. It was fundamental instruction in newspaper writing and I badly needed it."[57] On his first day as a part-time reporter for the *Jamestown (New York) Morning Post*, Frederick Palmer's city editor told him to find "something about our town that people in our town will want to read to-morrow morning, and our reportorial staff of one missed."[58] When Palmer returned with a story, the editor had him watch while he corrected it. A thirteen-year-old Moses Koenigsberg received the same, direct advice from Charles Merritt Barnes, the *San Antonio Times* city editor. Barnes told Koenigsberg: "Talk to everybody. Question them about what they have done and heard. Glean from them every bit of information that may be new or interesting. Then write up what you believe we should publish."[59] His education continued at the *New Orleans Truth*, where Koenigsberg turned in a story about a prize fight, but did not quote sources. The city editor explained that observations made by sources and included in stories must be attributed.

City editors could be tyrants, as Cobb discovered while working for Charles E. Chapin, city editor of the *New York Evening World*. Chapin courted the rich and celebrities with "flattering write-ups which, as supervisor of the news streams, he could smuggle into type."[60] Chapin often forced Cobb, by then an experienced reporter but new to the *World* staff, to collaborate in these efforts.

Besides teaching the basics of reporting when possible, city editors functioned as boundary spanners by enforcing style and content differences with competing newspapers. Dailies had their own "quirks" or idiosyncrasies of style, lists of forbidden practices known as "indexes expurgatorius," and sacred cows. City editors in their capacity as boundary spanners were partly responsible for enforcing these rules. Fads that had to be managed also were common. For instance, *Kansas City Times* reporters experimented for a while with news stories that began with verse. In New York City, some newspapers began stories with a single word or single line ending in an exclamation point.[61]

Russell also encountered sacred cows during his first job at the *New York Commercial Advertiser*; he referred to them collectively as the newspaper's "general steering chart" or "policy" chart.[62] The *Advertiser*'s sacred cows were enumerated on a list kept in a desk drawer by the night city editor. The list included four categories: People who must not be mentioned in the newspaper; people who could be mentioned only in a positive light; institutions or businesses that must be treated with care; and causes that the newspaper supported. More effective than the night city editor's list was the method by which editors and publishers communicated it. Cubs learned from the tone of editorials, from verbal messages, and more rarely upon written instructions how the business management of the newspaper wanted the lists to be used. Application of the steering chart to a story would be indicated by a "paragraph added, a phrase turned, a point emphasized, another point obscured, a certain meaning injected into a headline, a certain impression upon the mind of the reader not justified by the facts; and to anyone that happened to know the truth, an indelible conclusion of inaccuracy."[63] William Salisbury and William Allen White found similar structures for handling sacred cows at both large and small Kansas newspapers. At the *Kansas City Times*, Salisbury discovered some topics could not be written about and others had to be written about as dictated by the city editor, who in turn received his instructions from the publisher or managing editor. In smaller news markets, White learned county commissioners rarely were criticized because they controlled the contracts for printing the counties' legal notices. "At the weddings of their [commissioners] daughters, we printed the full list of gifts. At the funerals of their families we turned black rules of sorrow. If they dallied with the public funds, we defended them against the onslaughts of the less favored newspapers in the county," he wrote.[64]

Unlike Mencken's experience, editors and senior reporters generally did not have sufficient time to systematically tutor beginning reporters. Cubs often learned the rest by comparing the stories they submitted to the edited versions appearing in the newspaper or to the version published by competing newspapers. This "observation and imitation" approach was used by many. At the *World*, Jordan "watched the star reporters in the city room and studied their style and methods. I read every line in the *World* every morning, and as many of the big stories in the rival newspapers as I had time for."[65] Kelly did the same while working on space at a Chicago newspaper. Henry H. Klein was exposed repeatedly to how a story should be structured as he used a typewriter to take dictation from *World* reporters who phoned in ten to twenty items to him each night.[66]

Some editors posted examples of the types of stories they wished their staffs to write and the rules they hoped reporters would follow while polishing them. *New York World* city editor Morrell Goddard clipped what he considered to be exceptional stories from the morning edition and posted them in the city room. Goddard's colleague at the *St. Louis Post-Dispatch*, John Magner, likewise posted these successful efforts by *World* reporters. Such examples were rare, and reporters paid attention to them.[67] At the *New York Herald*, an exceptional story was known as a "peacherino." Stephen Bonsal produced his first peacherino about a dog fight. In his memoirs, Bonsal confessed: "In the style of the *Herald* of that day you had to read fifteen hundred words before you learned that while men were involved as accessories it was really a dog-fight, but as the desk men said, 'interest and uncertainty were sustained to the very end.'"[68] The *Herald*'s London-based publisher read the story, sent a copy to New York City marked "Good," and then summoned Bonsal to London.

Besides the city editor, cubs could learn from senior reporters who worked for the same newspaper, either by watching how they gathered news and wrote stories or by soliciting advice. A nineteen-year-old William Salisbury found the direct approach did not always work at the *Kansas City Times.* He eavesdropped on the veteran reporters' conversations "for pearls of wisdom," but admitted as a cub reporter he generally was despised.[69] Sometimes, the needed instruction came too late. Thomas—while a cub at the *Post-Dispatch*—was assigned to investigate a missing girl. He interviewed the mother, got a photograph, recognized the girl on a street car, and returned her to her mother's house. Both the city and managing editors were unhappy with his performance, but did not explain why. A more experienced reporter later explained that the incident could have provided the newspaper with several days' worth of exclusive stories if Thomas had not quickly reunited mother and daughter. There was precedence for similar behavior. The experienced journalist told Thomas of a reporter who had been praised by his editors for hiding the body of a dead man which he found on a deserted street.[70] The reporter wrote several stories about the man's disappearance, the search for him, and the final resolution of the mystery when the reporter "discovered" the body.

Cubs also found mentors outside the city room but within the building that housed their newspapers. While working as an assistant proofreader at a Buffalo, New York, newspaper, Blythe was tutored by his supervisor on the weaknesses of each reporter. Alexander Noyes said his interactions with the *New York Commercial Advertiser*'s proofroom foreman, an Oxford graduate, improved the precision of his writing. A tramp typesetter introduced Russell to the rudiments of reporting and layout. Russell benefited from another mentoring arrangement later in his career. While managing editor of a Detroit newspaper, Russell unwittingly hired Ross Raymond, a con artist who gave Russell "hints and suggestions about news stories that showed he knew my job better than I knew it myself."[71] Raymond had been the star reporter in 1876 for the *New York Herald* before embarking on his crime career. Russell later encountered Raymond while he was an inmate at Sing Sing. He once more gave Russell many practical suggestions about New York newspaper work. Irwin likely would not have survived his first assignment covering a trial for the *San Francisco Chronicle* without the aid of a staff artist, who coached him on what material was newsworthy.[72]

Some cubs were fortunate enough to cultivate these "star" reporters and famous editors through casual, social meetings that did not necessarily involve the direct transfer of workday knowledge, but that did advance their careers in other ways. Bonsal noted that he and other beginners at the *New York Herald*, who were indoctrinated with stories about the scoops of older reporters, sometimes received advice from these icons. Henry M. Stanley, for instance, was willing to give Bonsal guidance for handling their mercurial publisher. Bonsal also met war correspondents Archibald Forbes, William Howard Russell, and Richard Harding Davis. Marie Manning was a last-minute addition to a dinner party attended by Henry Watterson, editor of the *Louisville Courier-Journal*, and *World* managing editor Brisbane. She mentioned her desire to be a newspaper reporter, and Brisbane arranged a try-out for her. Eventually, she would follow Brisbane to the *New York Journal*, where she would invent the Beatrice Fairfax advice column. Marcosson had similar encounters with Watterson. Both men were members of the "Disreputable Club," an organization for theatre aficionados. Marcosson adopted Watterson as his model of the ideal newspaperman.[73] Ralph D. Paine idolized Davis, who had failed in an attempt to cover an insurrection in Cuba. Mimicking his idol, Paine organized his own attempt to slip into Cuba. He failed but chronicled his misadventures in newspaper stories. Shortly afterwards, he encountered Frederic Remington and Davis in Key West. Davis declared Paine's stories as "too good to be true—the delightful flavor of piracy—marooned on a lonely tropical key—and [my] thoroughly disreputable make-up."[74] Davis congratulated Paine on filing "first-class stories." In his autobiography, Paine gushed over the attention, calling Davis a "facile journalist and gifted story-teller" who had won early success.[75]

The work world beyond the city room also afforded the beginning reporter with opportunities to learn from other knowledge brokers—reporters from competing publications and the editors of publications that might buy freelance material from cubs. Poor pay often forced cubs to seek out freelance assignments from other types of periodicals as well as newspapers. The editors of these publications helped shape cubs as news workers. These relationships were particularly important for women, who found it difficult to overcome entrenched bias on the part of male reporters and editors. In an attempt to break into the

Chicago news market, Kelly discussed freelance story ideas with Helen Ekin Starrett, an experienced reporter attempting to launch a magazine in the same market. One of Kelly's ideas was an essay on how to use satire as an instrument of social reform. Starrett responded: "My child, those things will never do! No editor would touch them. You'll have to write about something you have seen, can describe, something no one else has done."[76] Rheta Childe Dorr's initial attempt to write for New York City newspapers as a freelancer succeeded because she met several "good natured writers who helped me with criticisms and suggestions, and through them editors were kind."[77] The story was different when she tried to secure a full-time job on a metropolitan daily in 1898. For the next three years, she sold "specials" for five dollars a column to Sunday editions of newspapers and other material to "cheaper" magazines before finding a job with the *New York Evening-Post.* Even though he had a full-time reporting job at four dollars a week at the *Chicago Record*, Baker found it necessary to freelance Sunday features for the *Chicago Tribune*, *Chicago Chronicle*, *New York World*, and *New York Sun* and weeklies like *The Independent.* He estimated that he wrote 70,000 words to pay medical bills from his wife's first pregnancy.[78]

Besides an extra source of income and instruction, freelance work could provide a bridge to a cub's next job. Baker learned that he could make more money writing fiction than news. Edward Mitchell, a reporter at the *Boston Daily Advertiser*, also wrote material for the *New York Sun.* He contributed a dozen stories and editorials to that newspaper before he was offered a full-time position. He eventually would be the *Sun's* editor.[79]

Freelance arrangements also taught cubs how to maximize their earnings from a single story. While a member of Yale's rowing team, Paine convinced editors at the *New York World*, *Philadelphia Press*, *Boston Globe*, *Chicago Tribune*, *San Francisco Chronicle*, and fifteen other newspapers to let him provide their coverage of Ivy League sports. His sports news syndicate covered his costs of attending Yale and paid his sister's boarding school tuition. Paine also discovered

> that the same news could be sent, by mail or wire, to several papers in different cities. This multiplied the revenue without increasing the effort. A poor but honest classmate who pounded a typewriter as a source of

> income was employed to make the requisite carbon copies, and at the end of the month the checks came fluttering in from hither and yon to make a gratifying total.[80]

White had a somewhat similar experience while attending a university at Lawrence, Kansas, where he freelanced for six newspapers and the Associated Press. Koenigsberg, who at an early age had witnessed a fatal shooting in San Antonio, admitted selling a stock story of several thousand words "based on those events and revamped as needed to 30 different newspapers."[81]

Cubs also could encounter knowledge brokers from a competitor's newspaper that were willingly to tutor less experienced reporters. These interchanges could occur both in the pursuit of a routine story or in a "pack" situation when multiple journalists pursued the same story. For instance, Cobb, the Paducah, Kentucky, correspondent for the *Chicago Tribune*, scored an important scoop because he received this sort of mentoring while he covered the arrest of a Chicago murder suspect. A reporter from a Chicago newspaper gave him background information from a previously published story about the murder; the circulation manager of a Louisville paper—an ex-reporter who had the evening off—helped Cobb structure his story. Cobb also had extraordinary luck in obtaining a key interview with the murder suspect. A guard at the jail at first rejected his request to interview the suspect, but the mayor of Princeton, Kentucky, the city where the arrest was made, had served with Cobb's father in the Civil War. The jailer likewise had served in Cobb's uncle's artillery battery. While officials said no one could interview the suspect and his accomplice, Cobb received permission because he was considered "home folks."[82] His only mistake at this point was using a large notebook, rather than jotting down information on "an inconspicuous wad of copy paper."[83] Chris Merry, the man accused of murdering his wife, "took pity on my greenness and gave me a better story than perhaps he would have given to a skilled reporter."[84]

This sort of interchange with knowledge brokers could take place over long periods of time and space and become forums on newsworthiness and ethics. The march of Coxey's Army on Washington, D.C., included both dimensions. Jacob Coxey, an Ohio businessman concerned with both unemployment caused by the financial panic of 1893 and his state's tattered infrastructure, organized the march. It was meant to convince

Congress to appropriate enough money to hire unemployed workers to rebuild the nation's network of roads and bridges. The marchers left Massillon, Ohio, on March 25, 1894. Forty to fifty reporters and artists followed 300 to 400 marchers, according to Baker, who accompanied the column as a *Chicago Record* reporter. The number of marchers and reporters fluctuated with the terrain. The press corps eventually dwindled to ten to twelve reporters as the marchers threaded their way through the Allegheny Mountains. That sparked a discussion among the remaining reporters about ethical behavior: What would be the best outcome for them—for the march to continue or for it to collapse? They eventually agreed that a successful march would be more newsworthy and discussed the possibility of using expense money from their respective newspapers to hire more marchers.[85] The reporters eventually decided not to intervene in the course of events, and the march continued until the last days of April when police officers stopped it as it entered Washington.

Not only cubs, but experienced reporters moving to a new beat within the same newspaper could benefit from contact with knowledge brokers. Lincoln Steffens, fresh from covering the bank panic of 1893 for the *New York Evening Post*, was assigned by his city editor to investigate police corruption. Steffens, however, had no police department contacts and found that reporters from other dailies had formed a cartel to cover routine police matters. They pressured Steffens to join their group, but he encountered Jacob Riis, who covered the police department for the *New York Evening Sun* without participating in the syndicate. Riis introduced Steffens to important police department contacts and also showed Steffens how to compete with the reporting syndicate. Rather than come to work earlier than cartel reporters in hopes of snaring a scoop, Riis had taught a clerk how to evaluate the newsworthiness of bulletins issued by the police. He and the clerk would sort the bulletins, and Riis would produce stories as needed. He also tutored the clerk in how to write basic news stories.[86]

Cubs needed to learn a vast reporting lore. Knowledge brokers in several guises could help by sharing knowledge through a system of interchanges or through journalism-related texts. Their tutoring, in most cases, would prioritize the importance of the successful interview with a reliable source.

Chapter Five

# Interviewers and Sources

THE ARTIFACTS CUBS consulted and the face-to-face interactions they experienced reinforced the importance of developing sources from every stratum of society, for executing the generic interview as the primary news-gathering tool, and for structuring the results in a specific format, usually the inverted pyramid. These skills represented basic tradecraft. More advanced skills remained to be mastered and learning them required the cub reporter to rely heavily on the "learning by doing" method. This was especially true for the interview-based story. Attributing a statement to a named source raised several issues. Overzealous reporters pursuing these stories could and did cross the line between private and public moments. Naming sources could require a compromise between reporters trying to give readers what they wanted and sources trying to improve their image or to sell their views. Writing the results of an interview often called for the same sort of finesse as found in works of fiction. The interview as a method of acquiring information, particularly for acquiring information from famous sources, also was evolving. No industry-wide conventions existed yet to address these fresh issues. Practices could vary from city room to city room or from reporter to reporter. How to get the story—or the interview that made the story possible—remained entirely up to the reporter.[1] According to some journalistic authorities the interview represented a contract between the source and the reporter. If the newspaper accurately reported a willing source's statements, then the source was obliged to stand by those comments.[2] Editors and reporters should remember that there were limits to legitimate interviewing.[3] Ideally interviews should be used to solicit information from public sources or "news of private persons in their public capacity," not as an occasion to invade a source's privacy.[4]

The news interview was an American invention.[5] Reporting developed in the 1830s, but it did not involve interviewing or, at least, the trappings of interviewing.[6] Historian Michael Schudson explained: "Much reporting remained nothing more than the publication of official documents and public speeches, verbatim. Reporters talked with public officials, but they did not refer to these conversations in their news stories."[7]

The interview, or the acknowledged interaction with a named source, developed after the Civil War. There were several reasons. First, public men found that the most efficient way to reach voters and consumers was by sharing their views and opinions through interviews conducted by reporters from the growing number of large metropolitan dailies.[8] "The men who act are to-day more than ever before, not the men who write," one reporter observed.[9] Sources also found the interview to be a safe way to test reader sentiment about public issues without personal risk.[10] If reactions were unfavorable, the interviewer could be blamed for misquoting the source. For the journalist, the risks involved in the named-source interview were worth taking for several reasons. Linking a name to a source increased the credibility of a journalist's work.[11] Capturing an interview with an important source—what Isaac Marcosson described as "big interviewing"—also increased a reporter's status among his or her peers. Finally, interviews were an important element of the popular human-interest story.[12] The trick for the reporter was to get the interview as much on his or her terms as possible.

In his guide book for beginners, E. L. Shuman described a rough dichotomy between the types of interviews. Ordinary interviews were meant to gather information from routine sources or eyewitnesses about news events. Drawn from the rank and file of society, these sources included bartenders, livery stable employees, barbers, tobacconists, railroad workers, undertakers, morgue attendants, hotel clerks, police, health officers, civic club leaders, and ministers.[13] In short, anyone who had routine encounters with the public fit into this category. Sources of this type usually shared information, but they seldom were identified in a story.[14] The other interview category sought sources among wealthy businessmen, society figures, or famous authors, composers, and actors. Shuman called these interview targets "public men."[15] Elizabeth L. Banks, a successful freelancer in the United States as well as Great Britain, referred to the stories resulting from these interviews as "personal write-ups."[16] Readers were interested in the private lives and opinions of these people, but reporters found that these sources often had to be pursued. Or, worse, they might seek to control the content of an interview in an attempt to gain favorable publicity. Reporter Marie Manning found that to be a key problem with some newsworthy women:

> A murderess, temporary heroine of the front page, was sure to speak of her canary birds. An old sinner of a woman, occasionally appearing in light opera when sober enough, told me that the stage had kidnapped her heavenly voice, but what she really enjoyed was darning stockings, making bread and watching little children play in the park.[17]

Reporters also discovered that Augusta Nack, the co-conspirator in the infamous 1897 Guldensuppe murder, quickly learned to use interviews to manage the public's perception of her.[18]

Coupling a source's name with a direct quote might increase credibility, but it also revealed the source in a way not used before. Some sources did not consider that a problem, but others protested that attempts to get quotes violated their privacy. Because practices differed from city room to city room, knowledge brokers and cubs could only share their experiences through CoP-type artifacts or through informal discussions. They learned that securing an interview with a nineteenth-century personage could require as much art, luck, and deceit as it did system. Work memoirs and magazine articles generated by journalists were chockablock with examples of interviews with ex-presidents, generals, and others that were nearly impossible to secure. These examples did not necessarily make it clearer what should take ethical priority—getting the interview or encroaching on a target's privacy.

Solving these interview-related issues usually called upon the reporter to be self-reliant. Late-nineteenth-century society was populated by difficult interview targets. New York politician Roscoe Conkling refused to be interviewed on any subject. James G. Blaine, secretary of state during Benjamin Harrison's presidency, would talk "only for publication with his most intimate friends" in journalism, and he insisted upon the right to revise his answers. Generals Philip Sheridan and William T. Sherman seldom would talk for publication. Frank A. Burr, who did the first postwar interview with Jefferson Davis, said editors like Charles Dana and Henry Watterson were just as difficult to interview.[19]

Writing freely of the just concluded second Cleveland administration, one correspondent complained: "To get information, especially from the Department of State, reporters function much like highwaymen robbing a stage-coach."[20] An unofficial policy of secrecy had been adopted by most government departments. Some bureaucrats would leak information, but only for their own benefit. Reporters complained that they did not learn important Department of Treasury news until it had circulated through Wall Street. Likewise, President Cleveland rarely talked with correspondents. He wrote his own press releases and had his private secretary distribute them to press association representatives on Sunday evenings. He believed Monday newspaper editions gave him more space. Washington correspondents hoped the incoming McKinley administration would encourage better press relations. There were indications that it would. McKinley had promised to meet with the press at established times, had been a guest at the Gridiron Club, and had told reporters to call on him and members of his cabinet for information on public affairs.[21]

When traveling outside of Washington, D.C., ex-presidents and famous generals made life difficult for the cub reporters often sent at the last moment to interview them. At the *New Orleans Item*, Moses Koenigsberg was assigned to cover the arrival of ex-president Cleveland at the railroad station. Koenigsberg was instructed to report only remarks made by Cleveland on arrival; editors assigned a second reporter to secure an interview. The former president, however, did not speak at the station, and he selected only one of the dozen newsmen present to accompany him on a carriage ride to a restaurant. Koenigsberg chased the carriage on foot. Cleveland admired Koenigsberg's persistence, and he gave the reporter an interview. Koenigsberg's city editor, however, refused to run the item because he believed competitors who had not acquired an interview would challenge its accuracy.[22]

While working at the *New York World*, Manning likewise was assigned to interview ex-president Cleveland about the advice he would give President McKinley about going to war with Spain. The city room's "supermen" had been sent for a week on the same assignment, but had failed to produce a story. By coincidence, Manning's calling card listed only her name, a name similar to that of the daughter of one of Cleveland's advisors. On the basis of this mistaken identity, Manning was admitted and announced that she was a *World* reporter. Reluctant to speak with her at first, Cleveland's compassion got the better of him when Manning admitted the interview was her first big assignment. She told Cleveland her employer might fire her if she did not secure an interview. Cleveland gave her a short statement advising people to be patient while the current president considered his options. *World* publisher Joseph Pulitzer sent Manning fifty dollars in gold as a bonus. She concluded from this successful interview that: "Good reporters sometimes fail because their reputation precedes them. The humble worm may crawl in where the soaring eagle finds a closed door."[23]

A *New York Herald* reporter assigned to interview General Sherman, notorious for refusing interviews and abusing news men, relied on novelty to get an interview.[24] Rather than face Sherman, the reporter tossed his handwritten question through the open transom of the general's hotel room. Sherman found the reporter's approach amusing and gave an interview. On another occasion involving Sherman, Augustus Thomas of the *St. Louis Post-Dispatch* paid a bribe to take the place of an extra at a theatre production that Sherman attended. Thomas got a story about the English stage manager's argument with American stagehands about who was the better general—the Duke of Wellington or Sherman. Sherman came backstage to greet the star during the course of the debate.[25]

Thomas's behavior was not an isolated incident. Stephen Bonsal, the *New York Herald's* star reporter for a time, paid bribes to get stories. For instance, he paid a guard to get access to the House of Commons' "Strangers' Gallery" to cover a story. Likewise, reporters could be bribed to do a favorable interview. Julian Ralph knew legislative reporters who took bribes, financial reporters who speculated in stocks, and others who were paid for writing favorable stories about people or events. Moses Handy, a *New York Tribune* correspondent, thought it worth mentioning that he did not have to resort to bribery or breach of confidence in 1875 to report the conclusion of the *Virginius* Affair—a dispute among Spain, America, and Britain about the fate of a ship and its crew used to supply Cuban insurrectionists.[26]

Although bribery by reporters and sources either to secure an interview or to obtain documents was not uncommon, some city rooms had strict rules against it. While at the *Sun*, Will Irwin was approached by a businessman who suggested a five dollar bribe be paid to a scrubwoman to obtain confidential reports about the Equitable Insurance scandal. Irwin asked the city editor if he wanted to pay the bribe. The editor asked Irwin what he thought. Irwin said he did not like the idea, and the city editor told Irwin he would have fired him if he had agreed to bribe the woman. Lincoln Steffens, offered bribes by businessmen to slant the news during his coverage of the 1893 banking panic, wrote: "When a desperate bear asked me into his office, offered to put me short of one hundred—two hundred—three hundred shares of a stock if I would publish information injurious to the company, I would leave his bribe to take, investigate, and, if true, print the news."[27]

If luck failed and bribes were prohibited, Elizabeth G. Jordan and Banks tried stylish tailoring.[28] When other *New York World* staff members could not get an interview with President Harrison or the first lady about their first grandchild, *World* editors dispatched Jordan to nearby Cape May, where the president was vacationing. Dressed in a white-linen, tailor-made suit, white canvas shoes, a white hat, and white gloves, she rang the doorbell. When the butler answered, Jordan asked if Mrs. Harrison was at home. Thinking the well-dressed Jordan was a family friend, the butler admitted her at the same moment the first lady entered the room with the grandchild. Jordan introduced herself as a reporter and was invited to spend the afternoon at the beach with the first lady and grandson. Banks, on the other hand, dressed well not to impress sources, but to impress editors. In her autobiography, she wrote having a reputation with editors as being a stylish dresser was important because they (editors) understood a woman dressed smartly can "gain admittance, get a hearing, and obtain an interview" where others could not.[29]

A cub or a recently hired but more experienced reporter might successfully improvise a connection with new sources when dispatched to cover a complex story, but those sources generally remained unnamed and provided background information. This benefited the reporter as much as it benefited the source. For instance, Florence Finch Kelly, Steffens, and Alexander Dana Noyes were thrust into situations requiring them to develop sources from scratch for specialized areas of reporting. In these cases, they had to serve as their own knowledge brokers. All three turned to public libraries, government reports, and trade press articles for background information. Kelly had lied about her credentials to get a job as an art critic at the *Boston Globe*. She admitted: "And

I, ignorant of almost everything pertaining to the vast and complicated subject, barely knowing the difference between a chromo and an oil painting, had boldly said I could handle the matter and now I had to plunge in and make good."[30] Rather than ask questions that would reveal her ignorance of the subject, Kelly listened carefully to what gallery owners and artists said.

Steffens and Noyes, neither with training in business or banking, found themselves covering Wall Street during a banking "panic." They had to pioneer their reporting methodology. Lacking sources, they found, required them to compromise. Steffens, employed by the *New York Evening Post*, developed a two-part solution to his sourcing problem. Like Kelly, he did considerable independent research to find background for his stories. Working from a list of half a dozen influential investment bankers provided by his city editor, he also asked if the bankers "would agree to trust and help me, not only to get but to understand the news."[31] In return Steffens promised to keep confidences and to not sensationalize the financial situation. The bankers agreed to the bargain, and they gave Steffens the names of other potential sources, including more bankers, brokers, speculators, and other financial specialists. These sources gave Steffens what he called a "good theoretical schooling in the stock and money market, as well as the daily news."[32] Rather than write dramatic stories about the collapse of banks, Steffens produced what he described as dull but accurate pieces. He concluded both the financial community and his newspaper benefited from the arrangement. Bad economic news was reported without sensation; in turn, the newspaper furnished readers with complete and exclusive stories. Steffens also avoided being exposed as an inexperienced and "ignorant" business reporter.[33]

Noyes, who worked for the *New York Commercial Advertiser*, had little knowledge of business. At least Steffens's father was a successful businessman. Noyes had withdrawn from the only business class he had enrolled in as a university student, and he had to ask directions to the stock exchange to cover his first bank failure. Like Kelly and Steffens, Noyes listened to sources more than he questioned them. He worried that asking sources to explain background material would expose him as an "ignoramus" and destroy his credibility. Noyes eventually found gathering the routine financial news was not difficult; much of it was publicly sourced. Noyes sorted out other stories about secret investment deals that could have important consequences later by tracking down the source of the rumors. Noyes eventually became an important business reporter for the *New York Evening Post,* then later the *New York Times.* He developed a series of rules for covering the stock exchange that he shared in his memoirs. They were: 1) Abstain from personal speculation. 2) Refuse all favors except those involving legitimate news. 3) Avoid physical presence at the stock exchange. 4) Choose carefully the people you affiliate with. 5) Judge every rumor by the source that shared it.[34]

For the cub reporter, finding a credible source and getting him or her to agree to an interview was only half the task. Successfully completing the interview, especially one that qualified as a news event in and of itself, was the other, more difficult half. Marcosson, who believed getting the facts of a crime story from a police officer was the toughest interviewing he had done, devoted thirty pages of his autobiography to explaining how he mastered interviewing skills. Interviewing nationally or internationally known persons required the reporter to know the subject's complete background including their eccentricities, hobbies or activities as well as their ambitions so that there were no lulls in the conversation. Others recommended a similar level of preparation.[35]

It also was important for the interviewer to inspire in his subject confidence that material which should not be divulged would not be divulged.[36] Besides presenting six rules for interviewing, Marcosson also reproduced seven others developed by Henri de Blowitz, the deceased Paris correspondent for the *London Times.* Several of Blowitz's rules exploited the subject's psychology. His first rule, for example, counseled interviewers never to leave a source abruptly after obtaining significant news. The interviewer should wait until the conversation has turned to the insignificant, thereby ensuring the source would not reconsider being quoted. His fourth rule cautioned interviewers not to reveal any preconceived ideas or bias about the topics touched on during questioning of a source. His rules included two specific to the reader: Never assume that the reader is familiar with the interview's topic, and, when writing for a nationwide audience, explain the geography involved. It would be unlikely for a reader in Oshkosh, Wisconsin, for instance, to know the location of New York's Bowery.[37]

Marcosson had additional advice for cubs who might encounter what he called a "non-imparter."[38] A reporter could use three strategies on a reluctant interview subject: assure them that they would benefit from the interview, convince them that confidential information would not be used in the story, and ease them into the desired topic by beginning with questions about a remote and unimportant subject.

Other news professionals explored how to manage the torrent of words that Marcosson's tactics might unleash. Charles Edward Russell, who eventually became city editor of the *New York World*, noted that sources might speak thousands of words during an interview, only a fraction of which were important to readers and journalists. It was the master interviewer's job to "seize in his mind the exact instant at which his subject began to say something worthwhile, and he must carry in his memory that utterance and all others of similar value."[39] The key points, presented in the characteristic way that the subject spoke, were to be reported. This required concentration on the reporter's part because note taking visible to the subject often "chilled" the dynamics of the interview, a point that Marcosson and others agreed with. A notebook indicated the reporter practiced "out-of-date, dry-as-dust journalism," Banks wrote in her memoirs.[40] Like Nellie Bly, Banks's reporting exploits made her somewhat of a public person, and women reporters often interviewed her. She recalled an encounter with a woman reporter she called a "model interviewer." Banks wrote that she had the "tact, the adroitness, the art of turning little incidents into entertaining 'copy,' and being a student of character and human nature, she had 'sized me up' most wonderfully well."[41] She contrasted that experience with an earlier episode in which a woman reporter had asked questions previously answered in earlier stories, had used a notebook, and had ignored in the story the fact that Banks spoon fed kittens while answering the interviewer's questions.

Russell believed that most public figures secretly wanted to be interviewed because it provided an outlet for those "full of a subject, or in dire trouble, or [who] has set the world agog by some uncommon feat."[42] Their initial reluctance meant only that they desired their lives and accomplishments to be viewed in a positive light. In those cases, the reporter had to balance the source's desires with his pursuit of news.

Preparing for "big interviewing" required nuance, and practitioners considered describing a subject's mannerisms and speech patterns as important as transmitting the facts of the interview. Knowledge brokers recognized that interview stories had evolved since the early 1880s. In old-style interviewing, the reporter asked a series of questions and usually noted verbatim the answers. In the "new" interview, Shuman wrote:

> What was formerly a dull broadside of set talk is spiced and enlivened by bits of description portraying the speaker as well as his ideas. Clever condensations of his words are made at points where he becomes too prolix, and droll side-observations are dropped in, while the monotonously recurring questions are often dropped out where the connection is clear without them.[43]

The reported dialogue should read like that found in a novel—exact words only are jotted down "on vital or technical points."[44] Cubs who consulted Shuman's book learned there were two ways to structure the interview story. The writer could start with a brief paragraph of introduction telling who gave the interview and where and when. Or, the writer could begin with the interviewee's most newsworthy comment.

Like Marcosson, the *New York World*'s Bly had mastered the art of inserting the side observation or "color" into an interview story. She demonstrated that expertise in an 1893 interview with three anarchists—Emma Goldman, Justus H. Schwab, and John Most. In the section devoted to Goldman, Bly began by describing her as most readers imagined. She wrote:

> You read of her as a property-destroying, capitalist-killing, riot-promoting agitator. You see her in your mind a great raw-bone creature, with short hair and bloomers, a red flag in one hand, a burning torch in the other; both feet constantly off of the ground and "murder!" continually upon her lips.[45]

The real "Emma" was tiny, barely five feet tall in her shoes, Bly reported. She had a turned-up nose and wore horn-rimmed glasses. When she met Bly, Goldman's "little feet" were "decorously" on the floor, and she had a copy of *Illustrated American* in her hands. She asked Bly: "'What is it you wish, madam?' I told her. I sat down beside her, and we talked for two hours."[46] Besides illuminating Goldman's political views, Bly informed readers that she was a dressmaker by trade, spoke Russian, German, French and English; and read and wrote Spanish and Italian. She had a private library of 300 volumes. Bly also made it clear to her readers that, on occasion, lying to a source to secure a story was acceptable. She, for instance, stretched the truth several times during her interview with the anarchists, and she shared those misrepresentations with her readers. While Bly inquired about the whereabouts of one of the other anarchists, a passer-by identified her as a reporter. Bly denied it, but inserted this parenthetical explanation in her story: "(I am called a special writer, correspondent, journalist, but in the strict sense of the word am not a reporter.)"[47] Her approach to Goldman, imprisoned at the time and unable to challenge what Bly would write, was similar. When Goldman told Bly she did not wish to be interviewed, Bly responded that she was interested only in Goldman's former life, not her current pursuits. Bly concluded the story's section on Goldman by writing: "And so I left the little Anarchist, the modern Joan of Arc, waiting patiently in the Tombs until her friends could secure bail for her."[48]

Even the routine, interview-based story could be infused with color like the following example from an 1899 *Chicago Tribune* story about a young woman who saved two newsboys from a team of runaway horses:

> Miss Lawrence is the 19-year-old daughter of Edwin Lawrence, an inspector for an insurance company. At her residence last evening she limped to the door and said:
>
>> It was not anything at all. I really did not know what I was doing until it was all over. But I felt that the two boys would be killed if some one did not get them out of the way. . . . What did the boys say? They only stood and cried. But then it really is nothing to make a fuss about, though I do believe that I would like to be a heroine.[49]

While readable and entertaining if properly executed, the interview story was a mixed blessing. Having sources did not necessarily ensure an accurate story would follow from the interview. Shuman estimated that nine of ten mistakes published by newspapers were the fault of sources. He recommended reporters check their facts with two or three different sources and "draw a mean from their extremes."[50] Philip Hubert wrote that mistakes often resulted from matching unprepared cubs to story assignments about "the distinguished foreigner as he comes down the gang-plank, the speculator as he retires from the Wall Street gambling-house with his million dollars, the actor as he leaves the footlights which have shone upon his first success, the clergy-man as he rests from the labor of a stirring sermon."[51] The interview, counter-intuitively, also limited what reporters could use in stories. Newspapers printed only a tenth to one-half of what they knew, one magazine contributor estimated. These self-imposed embargoes were used to preserve sources' confidence in news men and women.[52]

Finally, no industry-wide standard existed for what was public and what should remain private. The line between legitimate news and what should stay private is "fine—different newspapers draw the line at different places."[53] There was a class of reporters who believed in "no sacred home altars, or personal privacies, and that everything is legitimate property of which an item for their paper can be made" and who exploited the fuzzy boundary between public and private.[54]

Bias, intentional or otherwise, also could seep into interview stories, or reporters could expose themselves to influences that eventually slanted their reporting. Steffens speculated in stocks while covering the 1893 bank panic.[55] Reporters that covered horse races generally were permitted to bet on the races, according to "sporting" editor J. B. McCormick. He wrote that "men who bet on events that they have to chronicle are unintentionally influenced by their profits or losses, and their reports ultimately show it."[56] Rather than report on a race in which the reporter had a personal stake, these reporters should recuse themselves like a judge or jurors who know a plaintiff or defendant.

McCormick paraphrased Amos J. Cummings, one of the *New York Sun*'s managing editors, as saying: A reporter's goal should be to bring back to the city room "a pen photograph of what occurs, and not a distorted one, either."[57] If cubs were uncertain how to produce those "photographs," they could consult the models provided for them in works of newspaper fiction generated by knowledge brokers.

Chapter Six

# Career Models in Newspaper Fiction

BESIDES THE INFORMATION found in work memoirs, trade journals, and general interest periodicals, aspiring reporters found useful information in newspaper-related novels and short stories. These text artifacts included more than 300 items written primarily for English language readers and published during the last three decades of the nineteenth century.[1] Authors using editors or reporters as essential plot elements included Horatio Alger and Anthony Trollope. Many of these works about newspaper life proved misleading. Author and press critic James L. Ford found the book-length, "Park Row" fictions produced by others to be predictable. Their plots were the same and gave readers the wrong impression about journalism. In these stories, reporters wandered the city at will to obtain "'beats' of fabulous importance and 'show up' iniquitous bankers and statesmen."[2] The truth was different. The cub or novice reporter, if he or she survived their initial brush with newswork, would write and rewrite many more routine stories than scoops.

Present-day academics refer to these works as "newspaper fictions," "newspaper stories," or "newspaper novels." They are identified as texts in which reporters or editors are main characters and newswork routines like interviewing sources are main plot elements.[3] Karen Roggenkamp dates the appearance of this genre to the 1885 publication in *Frank Leslie's Popular Monthly* of "Scoresby's Mistake: A Newspaper Story."[4] Obviously meant to entertain the general reader, newspaper fiction also had other purposes. Media researcher Howard Good found the related texts published between 1890 and 1930 did two things. First, they functioned as a form of autobiography that informed readers about how journalists perceived their work. Second, Good discovered anecdotal evidence that these stories provided role models for young men and women considering careers in journalism.[5] Good's study also found broad themes embedded in the narratives: Journalism could be a school or a cemetery, a crusade, or an idyllic pursuit for country or small-town journalists. In the case of "Scoresby's Mistake," journalism was both an emotional and literal cemetery where the protagonist, T. Billington Scoresby, "boils down the locals, writes the patent-medicine puffs, takes charge of the 'spring poetry' basket, to relieve the literary editor, and makes himself miscellaneously useful about the establishment."[6] Unlike the stories and books that followed, "Scoresby's Mistake" is more an exercise in pathos than instruction in newswork as the hero discovers a decline in a co-worker's writing and intercedes on his behalf with the editor.

Some of the news workers analyzed here mentioned in their memoirs or other texts that they had read newspaper fiction and had been influenced by it. Particularly influential were Richard Harding Davis's *Gallegher and Other Stories*, Jesse Lynch Williams's *The Stolen Story and Other Stories*, and Elizabeth Garver Jordan's *Tales of the City-Room*.[7] H. L. Mencken, for instance, wrote that he read those three works as well as E. L. Shuman's non-fiction guidebook to newswork to prepare for his first reporting job.[8] While not all newspaper fiction was useful, the material produced by those who had been working journalists proved helpful to beginners in three ways, according to contemporary reviewers. These works furnished readers with authentic portrayals of city-room life, with fictional knowledge brokers who tutored both readers and protagonists in the basics of newswork, and with model career paths drawn in many cases with greater detail than those found elsewhere.[9]

A reviewer for *The Critic* summarized those points:

> Young people contemplating a journalistic career will do well to read these tales. They present the hardships, pleasures and triumphs of the profession faithfully, and incidentally give some information about methods and processes that is not without value. If all of them follow this advice, the book will have a large circulation, indeed, for the city room is the Mecca of numberless nimble minds at the threshold of life.[10]

The reviews exposed additional insights. Most of these fictions appeared to have been written by young men who had worked in city rooms just long enough to learn newswork, but not long enough to succumb to its vices, and many employed characters easily identified as actual reporters and editors.[11] Jordan's book was written from the female perspective, and reviewers believed her volume to be evidence that newspaper work was a poor choice of careers for a woman.[12] "Sympathy and consideration for the feelings of other people are serious drawbacks to the acquisition of news at any hazard," one reviewer concluded.[13]

For the most part, the fiction authors had sufficient credentials to act as knowledge brokers. Jordan arguably was one of the most powerful women in late-nineteenth-century daily journalism. She worked one year as editor of the woman's page at *Peck's Sun* in Milwaukee before beginning a rapid climb through the journalistic ranks. Between 1888 and 1890, she was a feature writer at the *Chicago Tribune*. She joined the *New York World* in 1890, working as a reporter and then editor of several departments before Arthur Brisbane promoted her to assistant editor of the *Sunday World* in 1897. Jordan became editor of *Harper's Bazaar* in 1900. She eventually became an independent author, producing thirty novels and story collections, the first being *Tales of the City Room*. Williams earned bachelor's and master's degrees from Princeton. From 1893 to 1897, he was a reporter for the *New York Sun*. He was a staff writer for *Scribner's Magazine* between 1897 and 1900. Like Jordan, he became an independent writer, winning the first Pulitzer Prize for drama in 1917. Davis served his apprenticeship at Philadelphia newspapers and the *New York Sun* before becoming the quintessential war correspondent—covering the Turkish-Greek, Spanish-American, South African, and Russian-Japanese wars for the *New York Herald* and *London Times*. He died in 1916 while covering World War I, but not before authoring a variety of non-fiction and fiction works including *Gallegher and Other Stories*.[14]

Kirk Munroe, who specialized in juvenile fiction, earned a civil engineering degree from Harvard, then surveyed rail routes in the West while writing a series of personal observations called "Letters from the Plains." Editors at the *New York Sun* liked his travelogues and hired him. Munroe dedicated his newspaper novel, *Under Orders: The Story of a Young Reporter*, to *Sun* city editor John Bogart. Ray Stannard Baker, the creator of *Pippins*, was studying law at the University of Michigan when he tried to make some extra money by writing. Between 1892 and 1898, he was a reporter for the *Chicago Record*. In 1898, he joined *McClure's* staff. James Otis Kaler was thirteen when he started work as a reporter for the *Boston Journal*. In 1864 at age seventeen, he covered the Army of the Potomac during the Civil War.[15] In the 1870s, he moved to New York and worked for the *Sun*, *Evening Telegram*, and the *Herald* before introducing a popular serial, "The Perkins Letters," about an American family trying to adapt to life in Paris, to the *Boston Globe*. Newsboys and bootblacks were stock characters in these columns. That the *New York Sun* would play a part in the early training of many of these authors is not surprising. Under the stewardship of Charles Dana, the *Sun* was known as the newspaperman's newspaper. Its editors valued the tightly written human interest story that reminded Will Irwin of well-written fiction.[16]

The challenges cub reporters faced in books and short stories by these authors did not frighten Mencken, but they did cause others considering careers in news to have second thoughts. A young Irwin, reading the same material as Mencken, was intimidated. He had considered careers in stage direction, playwriting, and journalism, but fictional accounts about newspaper work like *Gallegher* and *The Stolen Story* convinced Irwin that he would not make a good reporter. He wrote that "newspaper fictions" portrayed reporters as super-detectives able to force crooks, society women, and businessmen to divulge their secrets, scoring "sensational beats" in the process.[17] Before his career ended, Irwin, however, would make his own contribution to useful newsroom fictions.

Authors of workplace memoirs often identified their most important city room relationship as that with the city editor. Authors of fictional accounts, however, usually portrayed cubs' interactions with star reporters as their most important relationship with a knowledge broker. This difference possibly reflected the memoir writers' hoped-for relationship. Or, it may have reflected the notion that the skills shared in fictions by star reporters were more advanced than those learned in the city room or more dramatic in their application. In newspaper fiction plots, senior reporters helped cubs in two ways. A promising cub might be paired with a seasoned reporter to learn how important stories should be handled. Or, the cub might learn by observing a star reporter's activities either at his or her newspaper or at a competing publication. The knowledge brokers that the authors created sometimes intervened at critical moments during a cub reporter's career. For the most part, however, cub reporters in these fictions still learned the "considerable specialized knowledge" of newswork by experimenting, making mistakes, and reading the corrected versions of their stories after they were published.[18] They learned that speed, cultivation of sources, accuracy, and securing "beats," or stories exclusive to one newspaper, were the important elements of newswork. Newspaper fictions shared specifics about these goals and skills in great detail. They also incorporated the beginner-accessible examples that would be found in the textbooks used by the first generation of college-educated reporters.

Fictions and short stories also identified the four types of human raw material that knowledge brokers had to work with. There were those cubs who had followed the path from compositor or printer to office boy, then to reporter. The second category included better educated novices who hoped reporting would represent the first step in a literary career. A third category included older candidates who had failed at another profession and pursued journalism temporarily. The final group included: "Younger men, drawn into the life chiefly by the spirit of adventure, which a few generations ago would have taken them to sea, being sickened by the prospect of many monotonous days at a desk."[19] This category accounted for most of the cubs found in city room fictions. If they survived, these beginning reporters would fit in at Williams's fictional *The Day*, a "clean and clever" publication with a reporting staff composed of "self-respecting Americans, for the most part of good education and some breeding who did not find it necessary to lie or get themselves or others drunk in order to obtain news, which they wrote in very good English."[20] In other words, the successfully managed candidate would come most likely from a respectable middle- or working-class background, would have been educated beyond the grammar school level, and would not drink or gamble to excess.

The fictional reporters that cubs interacted with had formidable records equivalent to or superior to those of real-life star reporters. In *Pippins*, the *Chicago Times*'s star reporter, Keenan, "had been through half a dozen Indian wars and had brought back a long, jagged scar on his cheek as a souvenir of one of them. Every young reporter in Chicago knew Keenan at a distance, and worshipped him."[21] Munroe's creation, Myles Manning of the *New York Phonograph*, is fortunate to receive mentoring from the city editor and several reporters. However, he learns many of the finer details of reporting from Billings, who is from Chicago and whose iron nerves are well known. While others fled, Billings scooped up a bomb tossed into a crowd at an anarchist meeting and doused it in a barrel of water. Billy Woods, whose career knits together most of Williams's short stories, is *The Day's* chief correspondent and travels the world, penetrating "remote parts of India to write about the plague, Indian uprisings in the Badlands, discovering a new tribe in Patagonia" among other accomplishments before alcoholism ends his career. Ruth Herrick, Jordan's main character, mentors several women reporters at *The Searchlight* and travels the backways of Appalachia unescorted to secure stories for her paper.[22]

Fictional accounts also were specific about when cubs should reach certain benchmarks. Depending upon the newspaper, cubs must demonstrate their mastery of newswork basics sometime between their six-month and first-year anniversary at the newspaper. Beginners must start by covering the most routine stories like weddings and funerals or night assignments at the coroner's office, police court, and the city morgue. These assignments served three purposes, none of which required the beginner to write a complete story. First, the cub could function as a tripwire that signaled something important requiring the talents of an experienced reporter. Second, these assignments forced young reporters to establish sources that they could locate at odd hours and interview for information. Third, these assignments repeatedly drilled the reporter in extracting the same type of basic information from those sources, including "the age, address, initials, or occupation of someone in the story, or the name or precinct of the policeman, or the places or time of the occurrence, or the time or place of the arrest."[23]

Even a part-time reporter like Van Cleef in Munroe's *Under Orders* knew the importance of finding and interviewing sources. He tells Manning that a cub must learn to be friendly with all social classes "from presidents to janitors, and a good deal lower in the social scale than that too" in his quest for facts.[24] The goal was to make the cub as accomplished at interviewing as Woods at *The Day*. Woods is such a good interviewer he is referred to as a "genius" reporter. He knows where to find sources; he knows how to structure an interview to get what he needs; and he is an expert at getting "a perfect crowbar of a statement" from one important source that can be used to "prod and pry out the whole of the story, and without which he could have done nothing."[25] Woods's approach to a successful interview is instinctive; he does not follow guidelines found in non-fiction articles about newswork. Woods "had no rules about holding people's eyes or studying their weaknesses or addressing them frequently by name. He never planned beforehand how he was going to approach a man or woman: He knew how automatically," his co-workers said.[26] Woods also is known for his ability to make anybody talk, from busy bank presidents and crusty lawyers to East Side saloon-keepers.[27]

*The Searchlight's* Herrick also is a master interviewer. Assigned to question a woman accused of poisoning her husband, Herrick lays the groundwork by speaking to the woman's lawyer, writing letters to her, and sending her roses. These are approaches that male reporters, who have been sent for the interview without success, have not used. Once in the cell with the woman, Herrick realizes that conventional methods will not produce the interview she has been sent to fetch. Instead, she encourages the woman to think of her as an old friend offering to serve as a sounding board for her thoughts and concerns. This approach works so well that the woman admits she poisoned her husband after he beat his mother-in-law.[28]

The cub also must learn how to speedily compose a report conforming to his newspaper's particular style quirks without overwriting and without much conscious thought. This is not a simple skill to master. Manning, for instance, struggles to write four pages about a transit strike while Billings generates twenty in the same time period. Pippins learns to write his stories in crisp, short sentences, but he only discovers this skill while writing an important story under immense deadline pressure. Linton, a character in *The Stolen Story*, learns that he can let the story write itself. He ends his opening paragraph "as was then the vogue in *The Day* office, with a little short sentence. Like this."[29] Woods has learned to include with economy both sides of a controversy in his stories, but without letting his words indicate bias.

Finally, the cub had to punctuate this apprenticeship by securing and writing a "scoop" or "exclusive" whose merit is recognized by senior reporters or editors. Only cubs who have developed a "news instinct" or "nose for news" or "news judgment" could conquer this final hurdle.

News was "the wonderful, wicked, horrible—not the commonplace, the expected, the normal."[30] Detecting news required a reporter to develop a "habit of mind" or "an abnormal keenness in appreciating what is contemporaneously interesting to the public."[31] Even after a year, some cubs in these stories find it difficult to separate news from the mundane. Linton, for instance, cannot tell the difference. When dispatched to cover the reported suicide of a ten-year-old boy who drowns in the East River, Linton learns that the death is accidental. Returning to the newsroom, he tells the city editor that the death is a "pretty good little East Side pathetic story," but the city editor responds: "Hell, no. Hundreds of 'em fall in every summer. But a suicide at ten would have been good news, worth, perhaps, a column; for that is unusual. You see the distinction."[32] Linton finally develops a nose for news, but only after repeated cycles of trial, error, and correction.

Usually, the opportunity to score the requisite "beat" or "scoop" presents itself when more experienced reporters are occupied with other stories or when an editor decides to test a cub's resolve. To secure the scoop, the cub must demonstrate not only his or her nose for news, but also physical courage and character. Pippins of the *Chicago Ledger*, for example, is pitted against the *Chicago Times*'s star reporter, Keenan, when workers are stranded on a partially frozen Lake Michigan. Some are injured; others may die. The reporters race to the scene on a tugboat assigned to save the workers. Both have the story, but the tug's captain refuses to make the hazardous return trip to shore. Keenan attempts to bribe him, but Pippins manages a risky return to shore on foot. He is nearly frozen by the time he reaches the *Ledger*, where he writes his copy. It dominates the next edition while the *Times* does not have a story. The *Ledger*'s star reporter, Howard, simply tells Pippins: "You'll do, Pippins."[33]

Likewise, Williams's fictional Rufus Carrington gets his first important assignment at the *Star* because no other reporters are available. He is tasked with covering a press conference given by the Secretary of State, and his competition includes some of the city's best political reporters. Carrington knows little about politics; he has never covered a press conference, and the diplomat is known for an ability to baffle interviewers. Nonetheless, Carrington takes careful notes, and his story accurately reports the secretary's comments, which include an important assessment of national politics. Other reporters incorrectly report this key statement because they assumed they knew what the secretary would say. After careful vetting, Carrington's version is published, resulting in a scoop for the *Star*. The editor, who had planned to fire Carrington, now gives him a raise.[34]

Manning of the *Phonograph* has two weaknesses that threaten his progress—gambling and drinking. He also has two strengths. Manning has carefully cultivated sources in the rail industry. He also falls under the watchful eye of Billings. Because of his earlier stories about railroads, Manning receives an out-of-town assignment to cover an impending railroad strike. He manages to file an exclusive, but does not follow up with additional stories because of gambling and drinking. He even is charged with theft. Despite the exclusive, the city editor fires Manning, but Billings manages to clear his name. Conquering his drinking and gambling addictions, Manning is reinstated and eventually becomes the *Phonograph*'s leading reporter and later resigns to become a foreign correspondent for a prestigious, illustrated magazine.[35]

Characters created by Jordan perform some of the knowledge broker activities previously discussed, but Jordan's protagonists mentor women on technical as well as gender-specific issues. They also tell readers what stories should be avoided by women reporters. Herrick, for instance, has no objection to interviewing murder suspect Helen Brandow. Once it becomes clear domestic violence is involved, she decides to tell her managing editor that she was unable to secure an interview and warns Brandow not to speak to another reporter. Not only has Herrick sacrificed an opportunity to scoop other newspapers, but she has also placed her reputation as a reliable reporter at risk. Herrick, however, believes empathy as well as technical skills are necessary in journalism. When a recently hired woman reporter, Mrs. Ogilvie, falls short of expectations after six months on *The Searchlight*, Herrick tells the woman that her stories are harshly rewritten not because they lack "local color," but because they lack empathy with the sources. When Mrs. Ogilvie is assigned to write a story on an eighty-five-year-old woman whose husband has died, an opportunity dripping with human interest potential, Herrick coaches her: "Try to realize what it must be to her to face the world at eighty-five, with husband, home, children, friends all gone. Put some feeling into your work, my dear. Don't worry about the local color."[36]

As a knowledge broker, Herrick is equally adept at telling others what they should not do. When other women reporters gather at Herrick's hotel suite to discuss whether a woman, Alice Bertram, hired six months earlier, is an adventuress whose company should be avoided, Herrick argues that the woman's past is no one's business but the woman's. Bertram's past, however, would make a good story. She is the daughter of a wealthy mine owner, and she has taken a position at *The Searchlight* to win a bet with him. She has wagered her share of a trust fund that she can be more economically independent for six months than her two brothers. Not only does Bertram come from a respectable background, she also has been a good student of newswork. When the city editor learns that Bertram plans to leave, he offers her a raise. No one, however, manages to get the human-interest story about Bertram before she boards a train for home.

Jordan's short story collection includes one example of anonymous mentoring. Entitled "A Romance of the City Room," the story involves Miss Helen Bancroft, a relatively new reporter, and her unknown suitor, Hatfield, who sends Bancroft a dozen roses each week along with a critique of her work. He recommends books that will improve Bancroft's writing skills and makes suggestions about content: "Don't be too pathetic in your pathetic tales, he wrote once. Let your readers shed their own tears; and the memory of the terse comment was a fixed one, which strengthened her work materially."[37]

A third story in Jordan's collection warns women to avoid what Haryot Holt Cahoon of the *New York Recorder* called "wild-cat journalism."[38] This form of journalism traded on the shock value generated when a young woman journalist covered a non-traditional story, like a prize fight or a riot. One of Jordan's characters, Miss Van Dyke of the *Evening Globe*, falls back on this sort of journalism when a new managing editor finds her stories to be "correct and colorless little stories" that had no "go."[39] Fearing that she might lose her job, Van Dyke generates a story about an Election Day riot that pleases the managing editor, who assigns her to similar stories. A male colleague tells Van Dyke: "It was a horrible mistake for you to make. It's an assignment no woman should have taken, and no good woman would have dreamed of attempting it—if she realized what she was doing. I'm afraid it will take you months to live it down."[40]

Besides spreading basic journalistic knowledge, some authors used novels and short stories as platforms to critique news routines and professionalism and to examine the press's interaction with other institutions. Ford, Kaler, and Rudolph Block, the latter two often writing under pen names, built careers writing such pieces for *Puck*, *Life*, and *Cosmopolitan*. Ford considered American newspapers to be a magnifying glass that did not necessarily enlighten readers, but did distort reality. Rather than an engine of power, thought, and achievement producing accurate stories, the press too often relied on faulty routines that produced flawed accounts. He used one short magazine piece to lampoon "Professional Humorists" who spent their careers perfecting the art of writing "Crisp Paragraphs." In the same article, Ford criticized the newspaper practice of bylining contributions from celebrities—like "prizefighters, skirt-dancers, prominent citizens and other wind-bags, who had always regarded signed articles as their special prerogative"—while denying the same recognition to reporters.[41]

Reporters, in their turn, were naïve in their pursuit of stories, a flaw exploited by one of Ford's characters who sought to enhance his social standing. He is advised by a friend to enlist the aid of a reporter by telling him a lie that contained a kernel of newsworthiness. Once that story was published, the status seeker could follow up with more news tips. The friend concluded:

> There are a dozen papers in this town, and it seems to me that they're run for no earthly purpose except to publish a "Man-about-Town" column, or a "How-the-World Wags" column, or something of the sort. And what's the object of these columns? Why simply to make men like you and me famous. After they've made celebrities of us, they've got to go on writing about us every day; and when Sunday comes, you find our homely old mugs grinning at you from every printed page in the city.[42]

Ford did not hesitate to make his satires of newswork detailed enough that the victims of his criticisms could be identified. Less than a year after stunt girl Elizabeth Banks published her "In Cap and Apron" account of life as a maid in London households, Ford attacked her. In a parody published in *Life*, Ford created a male reporter for the fictional *The Daisy Chain* newspaper who had infiltrated the servants' quarters of a rich man's home. Ford wrote: "And would you believe it, although the only disguise he assumed was a striped vest, not one of the servants suspected that he was not one of them until they read his story 'Powder and Shoulder Knots' six months later in *The Daisy Chain*."[43] One of Ford's later targets was James Creelman, whose autobiography, *The Great Highway*, included a self-aggrandizing account of his role in covering the Spanish-American War for William Randolph Hearst's *New York Journal*. Creelman had been wounded during the fighting, and Ford recreated a meeting between Hearst and his injured correspondent that served as an indictment of sensational journalism:

> Suddenly a strange yellow glare lit up the scene and I opened my eyes to find Mr. Hearst seated by my side, note book in hand, while his corps of managing editors distributed copies of our blessed comic supplement—eight pages of roaring fun and frolic—among the wounded, adding to the horror and agony of the scene.[44]

The fictions also included accounts that celebrated capitalism in newswork. For instance, Davis's Gallegher is an office boy at the imaginary *Philadelphia Press*, and he possesses some of the qualities that a city editor might hope to find in a new cub reporter. He is street-wise and has a voracious appetite for crime news. Gallegher is personally familiar with many of the city's underworld figures. These connections with crime sources have made him valuable to the *Press's* police reporter. Gallegher is also a natural detective, and the *Press* has used him in an undercover operation to expose wrong-doing at a local orphanage. Playing the part of a destitute orphan, Gallegher observed what was going on around him "so faithfully that the story he told of the treatment meted out to the real orphans was sufficient to rescue the unhappy little wretches from the individual who had them in charge, and to have the individual himself sent to jail."[45]

Despite his past record, Gallegher is fired after he spends too much time with a New York detective seeking to arrest the murderer of a prominent businessman. Gallegher is undaunted. He arranges for a *Press* reporter and the detective to trap the suspect, but only after bargaining for a share of the reward money. In the end, it's Gallegher who must battle freezing temperatures and snow to get the reporter's notes to the *Press* before deadline. Once the story is handed over, the managing editor rehires Gallegher because he has secured a scoop.

Devotion to duty, capitalism, and chauvinism also are themes in Kaler's *Jenny Wren's Boarding-House: A Story of Newsboy Life in New York*. Though ill-educated and ill-clothed, the leader of the newsboys, Ikey Jarvis, sets an example for the others about selling newspapers: "Ikey was shivering on the corner of Ann Street, trying to dispose of two 'Heralds,' the last of his morning's stock. It was his custom thus to brave the winter storms, because he was the owner of an overcoat; he believed it to be his duty to remain out-of-doors during every business hour."[46] The boys naturally work their way through a series of misfortunes. They agree to finance a boardinghouse for newsboys with fifteen-year-old Jenny. A baby is abandoned on the boardinghouse steps; the boys work harder to care for it. Just as the boardinghouse opens for customers, all newsboys, the building burns. Jenny offers to sell newspapers on the street, but the boys tell her: "It can't be done."[47] The weather is far too cold to permit newsgirls to sell papers. Instead, the boys work harder and accept other newsboys as investors. Finally, one of the boys is arrested on a false charge of accepting stolen property. A lawyer client of one of the newsboys intervenes and secures the boy's freedom. Rather than receive his fee in cash, the lawyer prefers to use newspapers as currency. He instructs the boys to deliver the morning papers to his office each day for a week.

The newswork instruction incorporated in these narratives would continue to appear in Progressive Era novels, where more complex relationships between news workers and other institutions would be explored. Former *Sun* reporters and muckrakers Samuel Hopkins Adams and Will Irwin incorporated these complexities in novels.[48]

The knowledge broker in Adams's *The Clarion* is McGuire Ellis, previously the publisher of an East Coast daily, but now the associate editor of the *Worthington Daily Clarion*. The fictional *Clarion* is located somewhere between Chicago and New York, but the city of Worthington is large enough to support five other dailies—the *Banner*, *News*, *Star*, *Observer*, and *Telegraph*. Ellis's pupil is Hal Surtaine, the son of a wealthy patent medicine manufacturer who has used his father's money to buy the *Clarion*. He wants to use the newspaper to punish those critical of his father's business, but he lacks any practical reporting knowledge.

Surtaine has recently completed college and then toured Europe. While in London, he wrote and sold a few "sketches of queer places and people" he had encountered, but that is the extent of his training in journalism.[49] Surtaine's ignorance of newswork is large. Ellis observes:

> Together with the rest of the outer world, he had comfortably and vaguely regarded a newspaper as a sort of automatic mill which, by virtue of having a certain amount of grain in the shape of information dumped into it, worked upon this with an esoteric type-mechanism, and, in due and exact time, delivered a definite grist of news. Of the refined and articulated processes of acquisition, selection, and elimination which went to the turning-out of the final product, he was wholly unwitting.[50]

Surtaine's transformation into a responsible editor is gradual. It begins with Ellis telling Surtaine that there is no universal definition of news. "It's anything that interests the community. It isn't the same in any two places. In Arizona a shower is news. In New Orleans the boll-weevil is news."[51] Generally, Ellis points out, any person, place, or thing that is interesting should be covered in a timely manner by the newspaper.

Ellis explains that there are sources for news at the police department, city hall, the financial community, the local headquarters of political parties, at the railroad offices, in the theatre district, and in society. Reporters with specialized knowledge are assigned to those beats, where they get news that often is ready made for them. Not so predictable is what Ellis calls "the general, unclassified news of the city that drifts in partly by luck, partly by favor, partly through the personal connections of the staff. One paper is differentiated from another principally by getting or missing this sort of stuff."[52]

Ellis's conversations with Surtaine also are laced with other points of journalistic wisdom: Generally, cutting a story makes it better; the more tension, the smoother a city room functions; professional courtesy requires that scandals or libel suits involving other publishers should not be published. Ultimately, Ellis points out, what appears in the *Clarion* is controlled by a committee of local businessmen. They decide which newspapers receive advertising. Eventually, ethics dictate that Surtaine reject advertising from his father's patent medicine business and report truthfully about its operations. The book includes a token woman, who contributes a column by "Kitty the Cutie" to the *Clarion*. Kitty's "Lunch-Time Chats" are known for "their slangy, pungent, workaday flavor," and Kitty uses the column's popularity to campaign for overworked saleswomen.[53] Kitty, however, is not allowed to try regular news writing.

A volume by Irwin, *Warrior the Untamed: The Story of an Imaginative Press Agent*, acquaints readers with the different strategies—including exploitation of human interest value—press agents use to plant stories in newspapers. In this case, the press agent attempts to attract crowds for a new seaside amusement park in Massachusetts. The managing editors of Boston newspapers are not fooled by his various stunts, and one asks the press agent "in a Harvard accent if I thought they'd stoop to New York methods."[54]

Eventually, the agent decides to use the park's aged and toothless lion, Warrior, in a parachute jump. Surviving the stunt, the terrified lion flees the park, causing car and buggy accidents, interrupting a revival meeting, and terrifying sunbathers and shoppers. Country correspondents throughout New England now file stories about the "ferocious" lion, and homeowners arm themselves. It's a triumph for the press agent, who reports: "The first day I drew sixteen columns of space in Boston territory, and dozens more from the Associated Press—name of the park in every story. The second day it ran up to a cool twenty-seven. By Tuesday morning every man, woman and child in Greater Boston and vicinity knew that Paradise Park was on earth and doing business."[55]

Novice reporters, reading these newspaper fictions, were exposed to accurate portrayals of career paths in journalism. The path for women reflected their segregated existence in the newsroom. For the adventurous, women knowledge brokers like Banks shared methods for overcoming this segregation or for exposing it. Both men and women could learn the basic rules and routines of newswork from knowledge brokers functioning as roamers. Literary works by boundary spanners also exposed cubs to the concept of jurisdictional disputes with other occupations like the tale of Warrior or the *Clarion*'s struggle with patent medicine manufacturers.

The short stories and novels analyzed here included only one instance of deliberate journalistic dishonesty. That story, "The Cub Reporter and the King of Spain," appeared in Williams's collection and is an example of "faking" or publishing an "absolutely false" article with the intention to mislead the reading public.[56] In Williams's story, Hamilton J. Knox, one of the "least important reporters" in New York and previously a Princeton football star, decides to revisit the campus.[57] To pay for his train fare, he launches a false story about Princeton students and an unnamed alumnus who plan to burn an effigy of the King of Spain. Knox drops hints about the expected demonstration at the student newspaper and during a lunch with students. He leads the demonstration that night and drags the Spanish flag through the gutter. Knox then rushes to the Western Union Telegraph Co. office, files a story with his newspaper, and then rejoins the demonstration before returning to New York. The next day, his newspaper is the only one with the story, thus scoring a scoop. But students in Madrid launch a counterdemonstration and events quickly snowball into a real war. Offered an opportunity to join the press corps covering the conflict, Knox, who has found legitimate newswork to be too tame, resigns and joins Theodore Roosevelt's Rough Riders. He complains to a fellow soldier: "Newspaper work is no good; they don't give you a chance to run with the ball."[58]

Faking was a rampant journalistic practice during the final quarter of the nineteenth century.[59] It and other, like practices represented a code of journalistic "delinquency" similar to those found in other occupations. Newswork knowledge brokers would teach novices when to invoke elements of this delinquency code, and when to avoid it.

## Chapter Seven

# The Rule Breakers

WHILE RARE IN the city rooms found in newspaper fiction, autobiographies often mentioned acts of journalistic delinquency that represented a code of "rule breaking" standards that paralleled the legitimate rules of newswork. Reporters used these delinquent acts as a response to unfavorable employment conditions.[1] Besides guidelines for faking stories, these conventions included methods for sharing work among reporters from competing newspapers, for staging events with news value, and, in some cases, for abandoning an assignment altogether. Some of these acts of journalistic delinquency limited a reporter's ability to produce scoops as well as accurate stories, but the "rule breaking" strategies helped them manage workloads or earn additional income. Delinquent acts varied by market size and, in some cases, by the reporter's gender. For the most part, knowledge brokers seemed pragmatic about these and other practices that could be questioned as unethical.

Fakes were descendants of Penny Press hoaxes. Strictly defined, a fake was a story whose facts existed only within the story.[2] More commonly, fakes might contain enough truth that they were "not exactly lying."[3] Harmless fakes narrated past events using knowledge obtained before the event occurred or used circumstances or surroundings to infer how the event unfolded.[4] A more pernicious form of faking meant the publication of an "absolutely false" article with intent "to mislead an ignorant or unsuspecting public."[5]

Fakes in the last decades of the nineteenth century included stories that claimed the superintendent of New York's insane asylums had become insane and had to be restrained by a dozen people,[6] that an escaped circus lion had mauled and devoured a horse in a downtown New York stable,[7] that a story about recent fashion choices made by the first lady had led to the demise of the bustle,[8] and that the queen of the Hawaiian Islands was near death and the British navy was ready to seize control of the island chain the moment she died.[9]

Journalism was not the only source of fakes and faking in the Gilded Age. Competition in other occupations led to "epidemics of lying" that matched or eclipsed those found in newswork.[10] In the fine arts, for example, the demand from the directors of new national museums and private collectors for valuable paintings, prints, sculptures, and antiquities was so high that art dealers found it difficult to meet demand for popular items. Art historians sometimes refer to the century as the "golden age" of forgeries.[11] Some of the forgeries were so successful that their provenance escaped serious examination by experts for more than a century.[12] Demand was so high that "antiquities" factories opened in Odessa, Brussels, and Paris, and in turn were exposed by the press.[13]

Fakes in journalism had uses other than misleading readers. They could be employed to discipline sources or other reporters. Fakes sometimes were sanctioned by editors in smaller markets where readers believed their newspapers should entertain as much as inform. Others, like E. L. Shuman and George Grantham Bain, argued that "faking" could be a legitimate news-gathering strategy under some circumstances. They believed that preparing routine stores from background information and distributing them before the newsworthy event had occurred was permissible in regions where telegraph service was poor or sporadic because of the weather.

Shuman said faking portions of a story was excusable as long as that portion was about non-essentials. Most newspapers followed this policy, according to Shuman, who wrote: "Truth in essentials, imagination in non-essentials, is considered a legitimate rule of action in every office."[14] Whether this constituted a breach of ethics should be left up to readers, Shuman concluded. Bain, who defined faking as publication based on "the anticipation of events," openly discussed his more successful fakes.[15] He admitted that he had used faking while news editor of the United Press's Washington, D.C., bureau. In one instance, Bain instructed his staff to write a story about the upcoming wedding of a diplomat. Members of the wedding party supplied the details. This prewritten story was filed with newspapers with deadlines before or during the wedding. As a safeguard, a woman reporter attended the ceremony to check the accuracy of the pre-written story.

William Salisbury perfected the generally harmless "fake" during his nine-year, five-city career as a reporter. Editors knew about Salisbury's work, much of it done while he was the *Kansas City Times*'s "star" reporter. A favorite "fake" target was the city's Danish comptroller. Salisbury would concoct bogus interviews with the city official, mimicking his accent in print when he responded to imaginary questions. Salisbury delivered his masterpiece on a Sunday afternoon when the city editor, in desperation, asked him to find any story that would fill space. Salisbury's solution was a love story involving an Australian millionaire, his son, and the son's fiancée. The wealthy father did not approve of the woman, but father and son met at the train station in Kansas City and happily resolved their differences. They then conveniently departed for San Francisco on the next outbound train, sparing Salisbury the responsibility for writing a follow-up.[16] Before writing freelance stories about wildlife conservation for the *Boston Transcript* to pay his tuition at Harvard Law School, Mark Sullivan wrote what he called "fish stories" about an imaginary gang of criminals and a bear that stalked the woods near a small Pennsylvania town where he was employed as a reporter.[17] When a local police officer became uncooperative, Sullivan altered the officer's quotes to make him look foolish. In his autobiography, Sullivan explained that part of his job as a reporter was to supply readers with entertaining fakes as well as to use fakes to discipline obstinate sources.[18]

*New York Sun* reporter Julian Ralph, who hoped his memoir would be used as a textbook, employed the same device to punish an unpopular reporter. Ralph and several other New York reporters had been sent to cover the hanging of strikers in Pennsylvania. Ralph told the unpopular reporter that townspeople feared there would be an attempt to free the prisoners. This information was not true, but it had consequences. The unpopular reporter filed a story. He also spread rumors about the expected jailbreak to the town's citizens, who armed themselves. An unrelated disturbance in a railyard alarmed everyone who expected a jailbreak, and the reporters were obliged to cover the incident. Ralph observed in his autobiography that his practical joke in the form of a fake had turned into legitimate news he had to cover.[19] A fake also backfired on Florence Finch Kelly at the *Boston Globe*. Sent to cover a ball for working-class Bostonians, Kelly, who hoped to escape writing society stories, wrote an inflated account of the event. She reasoned that the exaggerated story would convince the managing editor to prohibit her from covering similar events. However, he was delighted with Kelly's work and assigned her to many more society events.[20]

Even with the best of intentions, those who faked the news—in part or in whole—were often discovered. Shuman recalled a colleague who had prepared a story about an expected meteor shower of "unusual brilliancy." It was a cloudy night; the deadline approached; the editor decided to print the prepared story. Rather than clear, the clouds thickened, and it rained. Shuman wrote: "The paper was the laughing stock of the city the next morning, and the enterprising editor had no need that day to feel of his neck to see whether his head was on, for it wasn't."[21] Samuel G. Blythe fell into a similar trap while working as a reporter for a Buffalo, New York, newspaper, but he was not too embarrassed to relate the details in his autobiography. Blythe had been assigned to cover a daredevil, Larry Donovan, who had promised to jump into a local waterfall. Donovan did not appear for six nights. On the seventh, Blythe played pool and filed a "Town Talk" column that asked the rhetorical question: "Where is Larry Donovan?" The next morning, the competing newspaper revealed that Donovan was in the local hospital after surviving his jump. The city editor reminded Blythe of the Donovan incident with each fresh assignment he gave the reporter.[22]

The professional consequences could be minor for even colossal fakes that initially went undetected by readers and editors, but sold newspapers. Kelly witnessed one at the *Boston Globe* when an assistant telegraph editor needed money for a train ticket. In his spare time, the editor visited the public library to research volcanic eruptions. Using his research and an imaginary interview with the captain of a freighter, the editor produced a story about the eruption of a volcano somewhere in the South Pacific. The captain, who had gone back to sea, was unavailable for additional interviews. The *Globe* purchased the story, which appeared on its front page. European newspapers and large dailies in the United States also traded the story. Eventually, the veracity of the story was questioned, and the telegraph editor was exposed. He successfully defended himself by saying all the material in the story was taken from "authentic scientific accounts" of other real eruptions.[23]

By the 1890s, faking had become so common in newswork that a contributor to *The Journalist* complained: "Not one in a hundred of these paragraphs is anything but pure fiction, coined at the point of the writer's pen."[24] He or she estimated that more than half the "specials" supplied to Sunday papers through news bureaus and press associations were fakes. J. B. Montgomery-M'Govern, who called fakes the "rottenest of all rotten journalism," participated in by only the ignorant or desperate, claimed women reporters were more successful than men at executing fakes. Montgomery-M'Govern said women had more fertile imaginations and were better at recruiting sources who would claim a fake was a legitimate story.[25] Besides the Sunday "specials" and the made-up stories that benefited "sources" that vouched for their accuracy, there was a third type of fake in metropolitan newswork that could best be described as extortion. This category involved a reporter making a deal with a source to write a libelous story and to file it with a legitimate newspaper. Once printed, the source would threaten a lawsuit.

Other forms of occupational delinquency like "staging" were harder to detect. Staging is not a term commonly used by nineteenth-century reporters and editors, but it accurately describes a story type closely related to faking. Like fakes and the crusades and stunts that would become hallmarks of yellow journalism, staged stories were exclusives or beats. Unlike the fake, however, staged news events could generate a series of stories that required minimal effort to report on the part of the responsible reporter. Blythe observed firsthand the serial effect from a staged story. The star reporter at the Buffalo, New York, newspaper that Blythe worked for purchased a hand and arm of a dead man from a medical student. He cut off several fingers and cut the arm into pieces. "Then he went out to Lock Sixty-Six on the canal and dropped in a finger, shortly afterward discovering said finger floating in the water," Blythe reported. "He came back and wrote a masterly story about his discovery. He speculated graphically on the problems of where the finger came from, whose finger it was, and why the police had not reported a missing man."[26] The authorities ignored the story at first, but the reporter continued to scatter more fingers and portions of the arm into local waterways and to write stories about the discoveries. Police investigators panicked, and the reporter finally wrote a story explaining the hoax.

Salisbury, who had proven himself the master of fakes at the *Kansas City Times*, proved equally able to manipulate staging. He repeatedly suggested to an alderman that the city council adopt an ordinance to ban smoking by those under the age of twenty-one. Salisbury, a chain smoker over the proposed age limit, meanwhile stirred up a public debate on the issue by interviewing doctors, ministers, shop owners, and others. He wrote a final story when the ordinance passed. Salisbury used the same strategy several times to generate stories. Kent Cooper, who worked as a reporter for Indianapolis newspapers and who later would be chief executive officer of the Associated Press for twenty-five years, found the carbon paper for a murder case deposition in a court stenographer's unlocked office. The contents of the deposition supplied his first story. An interview with the man who gave the deposition generated a second. Cooper explained how he had obtained the deposition in a final story. The master interviewer Isaac Marcosson staged a story involving Richmond Pearson Hobson, a naval hero from the Spanish-American War. Fans, mostly women, had mobbed Hobson after he gave a speech in New York City. Many of the women kissed him. When Marcosson learned that Hobson was coming to St. Louis, he recruited a local woman to recreate the New York City mob scene.[27]

"Combines" or combination reporting linked reporters trying to solve a common problem but operating from different city rooms. As a workload management tool, combines developed their own unwritten rules to govern members' behavior. Stories were shared, especially if an assignment was too complex for a single reporter to complete.[28] If a member could not participate for some reason, his colleagues from competing newspapers would file stories with his newspaper. Anyone who withheld information from the combine would be disciplined by the other members, who would work to scoop the noncompliant reporter. This treatment would continue until the offender was fired or transferred by his newspaper.[29] Post-Civil War coverage of the federal government illustrates why combines were needed. In 1886, reporters from about 125 dailies and twenty-five press associations covered Washington, D.C., from the congressional press galleries. The largest newspapers could afford to employ three men to do this work while Congress was in session. Most newspapers, however, could afford only one Washington-based special correspondent, who naturally found it impossible to cover all the news. This reporter would combine his reporting with that of two, three, four, or as many as six other reporters by sharing stories.[30] There also were those special correspondents who combined several client newspapers, sharing the same stories with all of them. According to "Seyon," the pen name of a contributor to the *Chautauquan*, reporters from this category were the only ones who benefited from this arrangement. Seyon wrote that their work was inferior, but profitable.[31]

The "combine" reporting approach could be modified for regional and local conditions. For East Coast newswork, the combination approach applied to routine news, defined by Edward P. Mitchell, editor of the *New York Sun* for several years, as common property because all reporters had the same opportunity to obtain it.[32] Will Irwin found the same custom held true for West Coast reporters covering police, city hall, or the morgue. West Coast editors, however, were more likely not to approve of the practice. Reporters there secretly traded information and stories. Constant uniformity in which stories were covered also might alert editors to a combination, so reporters competed for legitimate scoops once or twice a week.[33] Neither reporters nor editors approved of combination reporting in small cities like 1880s St. Louis. Those communities were not large enough to attract a news agency that would spoil opportunities for easy scoops by providing the same stories to all newspapers.[34]

Reporters who refused to join a combine could be punished by other reporters as Salisbury was in Kansas City. Community leaders there left news notes on hooks in drug stores for their favorite newspapers. Reporters for three other Kansas City newspapers disliked Salisbury's enthusiasm for turning these notes into stories. They planted fake notices for him that he reported.[35] After several of these mistakes were discovered, Salisbury joined the combination.

Combinations could be defeated, but victory sometimes required outside help. Lincoln Steffens, for instance, encountered a powerful combination consisting of evening edition reporters when dispatched by the *New York Evening Post* to uncover corruption at the police department. His competitors began their workday between 8 a.m. and 9 a.m. by scanning the news bulletins posted by the police. The stories were split up; each reporter covered his portion and shared it with the other news workers.[36] Steffens survived without joining the combination partly because the *Evening Post* was not interested in routine crime news and partly because Jacob Riis from the *New York Sun* introduced him to the appropriate news sources.

Combinations functioned as long as the participants had latitude to develop the occasional scoop and shared the same news judgment. They failed when one reporter in the combination encountered a story involving his newspaper's "sacred cows." At those times, forming a partnership with a less experienced or less principled reporter could be hazardous, as Moses Koenigsberg learned while covering courts for the *New Orleans Item*. Koenigsberg's combination partner from the *New Orleans Daily States* failed to report a rape story. Rather than explain the missing story to his city editor, Koenigsberg joined the staff of the *New Orleans Truth*.[37]

There was one final strategy that a reporter might employ to avoid doing a story, but it was risky. Women, who aspired to reporting duties beyond writing society columns and doing stunt work, used this rule-breaking approach to avoid physically hazardous assignments and society stories and to protect their sources. Reporters tried to avoid these stories by telling editors that a critical source would not cooperate or had no news. This strategy required maneuvering a source into promising they would not cooperate with other reporters. Experienced news women like Elizabeth L. Banks also could refuse to do some assignments. Banks used this tactic so often that editors nicknamed her "the great objector."[38] The learning curve for Banks, however, was steep, and she survived to become a knowledge broker because she spent most of her career as a successful freelancer. As a cub, Banks was asked by a city editor to interview an actress who had forgotten her lines during a performance. Rumors implied that she had been drunk. The actress refused to see the first four reporters, all male, sent to interview her.[39] Banks, however, was admitted and identified herself as a reporter. The actress poured out the sordid details of her life, then asked Banks to keep the information confidential. Banks eventually agreed. When she told the city editor the bargain she had made, he said:

> I would dismiss you from the staff instantly for rank disregard of the interests of your paper. As you are a woman, I will say that you have not the journalistic instinct. You will never be able to do big things in journalism. You can edit your own page, but you'll never be a really successful journalist. The fact is you're all woman and no journalist.[40]

Banks made sure the sabotage of an assignment went undetected in another episode. She was assigned to join John Philip Holland for a trial cruise of his submarine. Considering the assignment far too hazardous, she dressed to emphasize a "frail, delicate, feminine appearance" before going to the docks. Holland reacted by refusing to take Banks on the test cruise. Banks made him promise not to take any reporter—male or female—on a similar voyage. Finally, Banks would not use information shared in confidence by a good source. She lied instead. Banks, for example, was dispatched to Washington, D.C., to interview an American diplomat. The two talked at length on many subjects during dinner. On the return train trip, Banks decided none of the conversation, some of which might have worsened international tensions, should be reported. She told her editor the diplomat had refused to be interviewed.[41]

Cubs undoubtedly learned these delinquent practices—faking, staging, combining, and others—the same way they learned the legitimate rules. They observed and imitated or learned by reading the memoirs of knowledge brokers or by reading fictional accounts. The delinquency code was another of newswork's repertoire of tools, solutions, rules, and other artifacts circulated through CoPs by the occupation's "roamers." It was an informal creation with only one, shared guideline: Punishment for delinquent behavior generally could be avoided if it produced an exclusive like the newsboy in Richard Harding Davis's widely circulated *Gallegher* short story. Otherwise, reporters often relied upon their sense of personal ethics. In his autobiography, Alexander Noyes wrote that ethics in journalism as well as society were crude in their simplicity during the Gilded Age while actual reporting was complicated.[42] For Banks and others, the complexities of newswork meant refusing any assignment they identified as immoral or hazardous. When asked by an editor to walk along Broadway at midnight until she was arrested for prostitution, Banks replied that she would if the editor asked his sister to complete a similar task.[43] Banks later wrote:

> When a woman was a newspaper reporter, where was the dividing line between herself as woman and as reporter? Should she govern her womanhood and her honour by her journalistic instinct, or should she govern that journalistic instinct by that honour and that womanhood?[44]

For Ralph, it meant taking extraordinary steps to secure an important story and then consulting his conscience about the suitability of those steps. He wrote that only journalists could determine whether the methods they employed to secure a story were ethical.[45]

Incidents of delinquent behavior, like those James L. Ford attacked in his satires, did raise questions about what constituted ethical conduct. Should a code of ethics govern the reporter's work relationship with audiences, with editors and publishers, with sources, or with other reporters? Should the reporter's own conscience be the primary guide to ethical conduct in these relationships? Which relationship had priority? The search for answers to such ethical questions usually focused on the editor-audience or reporter-source relationships and appeared in trade or general interest periodicals. Some of these essays had been thoughtfully prepared. For instance, Harry Thurston Peck, an accomplished academic who had switched careers to edit the *New York Commercial Advertiser* and the *Bookman*, wrote that most critics missed three important flaws in American journalism. These shortcomings were not inaccurate reporting, sensation-mongering, and invasion of privacy, all of which had ethical ramifications. Peck explained that journalism lacked nonpartisan reporting of politics, suffered from a preoccupation with "localism," and needed to understand that it would soon be asked to cater to a new audience. Localism meant newspapers' preoccupation with covering only those stories that occurred within one hundred miles of their pressrooms. This sort of content would not satisfy the growing audience of middle-class workers from new occupations generated by post-Civil War industrialization. These "trained and thoroughly intelligent men" would not be influenced by cheap jokes, tawdry rhetoric, and big headlines.[46] Peck hoped they would be the readers for a new, national newspaper.

Editors also carried a special burden for ethical behavior since in many communities newspaper circulation exceeded church attendance, a *Fourth Estate* contributor wrote. Unfortunately, editors had no other code of ethics to guide them than public opinion and their own conscience. "They do not have to pass an official examination for admission to their profession, like that which lawyers must undergo for admission to the bar. They are not bound by the oath and the legal restrictions which bind the practitioner of medicine. They are under no authority like that which the church exercises over its ministers."[47]

*The Journalist*, which frequently addressed ethical issues, focused on the relationship between reporters and sources. Its "Hints to Journalists" column treated common missteps in that relationship with satire. "In case of being engaged in working up a particularly disagreeable story, if you are offered ten dollars to keep anybody's name out of the paper, indignantly refuse. You might get twenty," one column concluded.[48] Another suggested: "All reporters should write to theatrical managers for free tickets. They cannot do anything for the managers, but at the same time men who run theatres love to give passes to useless people. Never neglect this work when theatres are full."[49]

Others blamed ethical shortcomings on the business practices used for hiring editors or for paying reporters. It was not unusual for inexperienced men to be hired by newspaper stockholders for news management positions because of their social or economic connections. Beneficiaries of this hiring process could be seen every day "dictating rules to and criticizing the work of old, able, experienced and accomplished reporters."[50] These city and managing editors retained their positions because they were shrewd enough to hire competent subordinates. Other critics believed payment practices and other city-room routines caused ethical or performance breaches. John Brisben Walker, who founded *Cosmopolitan* in 1893, blamed the practice of paying reporters on space—or for the amount of a story that appeared in print—for many of journalism's ethical problems. This method of payment began to appear in the 1870s, and it changed reporting practices. Walker wrote that "truth" takes a place in the background in this system because: "It is not really to the advantage of the space-writer to adhere carefully to bare facts. It is to the interest, and it is the business, of the news editor to have truth; but his staff is organized in a way to prevent its acquisition."[51] The space system trapped reporters between the editors charged with cutting and correcting their stories and the reporter's need to produce copy, accurate or not, that the newspaper would print. The system turned writing into a "gamble" for reporters and encouraged them to adopt "shiftless habits."[52] Besides pay, other employment practices also taxed reporters. Some city editors required a reporter on morning newspapers to wait long hours alone in the city room to make sure no newsworthy events occurred before the edition was printed. The same reporter might be required to work the next day without adequate rest.[53]

These examples suggest three categories of ethical decision-making existed or were developing: 1) Nineteenth-century reporters who covered highly specialized areas like finance or sports understood that their work required a common code of behavior. In the absence of one, reporters created their own rules for interacting with sources who often were their primary readers. 2) Reporters covering stories of a general nature valued ethical relationships with other reporters. Like members of a CoP, they willingly debated what rules they should follow as a group, much like in combination reporting. 3) In the absence of a CoP-like discussion, reporters relied on their own, personal code of ethics to guide their relationships with sources, editors, and other reporters.

Banks, perhaps because she often worked alone as a freelancer, represents the third category. As shown above, when an editor asked her to use her gender to secure an interview with the actress, Banks successfully completed the task, but then refused to write the story because she felt it unfair. Asked to take a cruise in Professor Holland's prototype submarine, she decided the physical risk was too great. Instead, she lied to both her source and her editor to escape the assignment. Koenigsberg, lacking adequate supervision for the early portion of his career, compiled his own code for ethical newswork. He later used his autobiography to circulate his code. When covering the same story, reporters in the second category could interact and develop a joint solution without input from supervising editors. Ray Stannard Baker encountered this work community response while covering the march of Coxey's Army. As the number of marchers dwindled, the reporters considered using expense account money to hire more marchers to inflate the story's importance, but decided not to. A march organizer, disgruntled with the stories being produced, began referring to the press corps as the "Forty Argus-Eyed Demons of Hell." Rather than alter their reporting to punish the march's leaders, the correspondents responded in kind by referring to themselves as the "Argus-Eyed Demons of the Commonweal of Correspondents."[54]

Specialty reporters primarily were concerned with two relationships—with readers whose livelihood depended upon the accuracy of their reports and with sources who supplied the facts that they used. Chapter 5 provided examples of how three reporters, Steffens, Noyes, and J. B. McCormick, struck this balance. Steffens and Noyes were assigned to cover a bank panic; neither had sources or experience with financial reporting. At the end of their ordeal, both suggested guidelines for covering volatile financial news. Noyes's suggestions were in the form of rules for ethical behavior, especially how to avoid being co-opted by sources. McCormick, a sports reporter and editor, also warned reporters that they would best be served by not betting on sports events they covered. Business, sports, and other specialized areas of reporting also required that reporters be able to present complex information in a form that could be understood by ordinary readers. The great masses that read newspapers had "only a limited elementary education," but they read newspapers for instruction as well as news and were entitled to both.[55]

The rules for detecting, procuring, and writing news were similar from city room to city room, but the guidelines for ethical behavior still required refinement along the lines offered by Koenigsberg. Despite a rocky start as a reporter in San Antonio, Koenigsberg had steadily climbed journalism's career ladder. He joined William Randolph Hearst's publishing empire in 1903 as managing editor of the *Chicago American*. He became president of the International News Service, Cosmopolitan News Service, Premier Syndicate, and the Star Adcraft Service. He built an international reputation as a free press advocate and compiled "A Newspaperman's Seven Commandments" that appeared in his autobiography. Commandment Four addressed journalistic ethics: "At all times and in all things the editor must serve the reader to the exclusion of everyone else."[56]

## Chapter Eight

# Conclusion

THE COMMUNITIES OF Practice model offers a new way to organize answers to old questions: What did cub reporters learn about newswork? How did they learn it? Who taught them in the absence of university professors and curricula, textbooks, and formal apprenticeship programs? Considering the work histories of the news workers profiled here, however, a more tempting question might be: How could a novice reporter during the last decades of the nineteenth century avoid learning the essentials of newswork?

During those decades, knowledge brokers filled a variety of conduits with information about how to perform various news tasks. Those knowledge agents shared the key attributes identified in CoP research. They had been exposed to new practices for solving work problems; they had the necessary mobility to share those solutions within a CoP or across a constellation of CoPs, and they also had created durable and informative work "artifacts" encapsulating newswork information. They shared that information through guide books, autobiographies, trade journals, face-to-face interactions, novels, general interest periodicals, and short stories. Some novices, like H. L. Mencken, complained that these resources were rare, but he managed to find and read E. L. Shuman's guide book and several newspaper fictions. Mencken's city editor in Baltimore also carefully tutored him in the basics of newswork. In New York, Henry Klein felt he had received sufficient instruction just through reading competitors' newspapers and by using a typewriter to record each night ten to twenty stories phoned in to his city room by more experienced reporters. In smaller markets, the opportunities to learn may have been more constrained, but not completely absent. For instance, Moses Koenigsberg operated by trial and error until the city editor for a New Orleans newspaper mentored him.

For many young reporters, opportunities existed for simultaneous tutoring by multiple knowledge brokers. These opportunities often came in the guise of freelance assignments and could be as basic as comparing the story they wrote to the story that was published. Ray Stannard Baker learned that way while working at the *Chicago Record*, which had no Sunday edition. Consequently Baker freelanced Sunday features for the *Chicago Tribune*, *Chicago Chronicle*, *New York World*, *New York Sun*, and weekly publications like *Outlook* and *The Independent.* Florence Finch Kelly studied the work of her competitors while covering society events on a part-time basis for a Chicago newspaper. At the same time, she solicited practical advice from women reporters like Annie Diggs of the *New York Tribune* and from E. P. Baker, editor of the *Topeka Commonwealth,* who had given Kelly her first city-room job. As a student at Yale, Ralph D. Paine worked for as many as twenty newspapers including the *New York World*, *Philadelphia Press*, *Boston Globe*, *Chicago Tribune*, and *San Francisco Chronicle.*

"Newspaper fictions" also created CoPs in the form of fictional city rooms. These imaginary work communities included knowledge broker-type characters who tutored fictitious cubs. The brokers, in the case of Kirk Munroe's and Samuel Hopkins Adams's books, came from other news markets and were successful in their present assignments. They had legitimacy. In often informal settings like casual conversations on the street, they passed along useful information about what was and was not news, where news could be obtained, useful guidelines for producing the story text, and the time frame for reaching career benchmarks, something not so carefully spelled out by non-fiction sources. Their fictional students, at first blank slates requiring constant monitoring and instruction, eventually became successful reporters.

The knowledge brokers who tutored cubs directly or indirectly could do so as boundary agents, outposts, or roamers. Boundary spanners like Charles Rosebault at the *New York Sun* performed maintenance work along his CoP's borders by teaching and reinforcing accepted rules and routines. Others like Arthur Brisbane acted as "roamers" who moved one step higher on the ladder of journalism with each new job while simultaneously advancing the careers of a cortege that included Marie

Manning and Elizabeth Garver Jordan. Finally, Frank O'Brien, with his multiple departures and returns to the *Sun* city room, fulfilled the outpost's role of exploring new areas only to return later to his home CoP, where he could share that information.

The availability of information and mentors to teach was not the problem for the nineteenth-century cubs studied here, atypical though they might have been. The fluidity and complexity of the information was. The rules of newswork came in several different categories: "Mechanical" or "academic" rules, idiosyncratic standards, and rules governing acceptable, but "delinquent" acts. Editors and reporters also added new rules or routines as the content formulas used by their newspapers changed.

"Mechanical" rules constituted the basics of newswork and generally were the same from one city room to the next. Besides identity-fixing nomenclature and grammar, mechanical rules covered how to locate potential news sources, how to interview those sources for news, and how to structure a basic news story. Irvin Cobb believed it essential that beginners learn these rules so that they knew "when and where to break them" to produce a more readable story.[1] Idiosyncratic rules varied from newsroom to newsroom and included indexes expurgatorius, fads, and sacred cows, all accorded special treatment by a newspaper. Reporting fads also needed management. For instance, some newspapers would start every story with a line or two of verse; others would begin crime stories with a single word like "Robbed!" Indexes expurgatorius usually included an editor's interpretation of the rules of grammar like whether to use "off of" or "off." Finally, editors and reporters also drafted guidelines for producing fresh types of news like the increasingly popular human-interest story.

The academic or mechanical rules found their way into early journalism textbooks issued in the first two decades of the twentieth century.[2] Journalists turned academics usually wrote these texts. Authors included Charles G. Ross, Grant M. Hyde, Harry Franklin Harrington, Theodore Thomas Frankenberg, Willard Grosvenor Bleyer, and M. Lyle Spencer.[3] Frankenberg had been a sub-editor at the *Columbus Dispatch* and a drama critic at the *Columbus Citizen* and *Ohio State Journal*. Harrington, who also had worked for the *Ohio State Journal* and other Ohio newspapers, was the director of Ohio State University's journalism courses. Hyde, who taught journalism at the University of Wisconsin, had been managing editor of *Popular Science Monthly* and on the staff of the *New York Evening Mail.* Spencer, an English professor at Lawrence College in Appleton, Wisconsin, earlier worked as a reporter, copyreader, and editorial writer for the *Milwaukee Journal.* Bleyer's experience was confined to working for University of Wisconsin publications, including the editorship of the *Daily Cardinal.* Ross, an assistant professor of journalism at the University of Missouri, had reported for the *St. Louis Post-Dispatch* and *St. Louis Republic.*[4]

The content of textbooks by these and other authors had some strong similarities to the guide books and other sources of information produced in the last quarter of the nineteenth century. All contained a chapter on how to structure a news story. Four included chapters on conducting interviews, defining news, discussing news values, and explaining other methods for gathering information. Four also included chapters or appendices explaining the nomenclature used in a city room and the differences between standard English and newspaper English. The textbooks still recognized differences in interviews. Reporters still could take some liberties in sketching a subject's personality in the type of interview that qualified as a news event in and of itself, but he or she could not do the same while conducting interviews to obtain facts about newsworthy events. The authors devoted little space to terms associated with ethical or legal issues like "faking," "fairness," "bribery," or "suppression" of the news.

Textbook writers and late-nineteenth-century reporters and editors appeared to be ambivalent, for the most part, about ethics. Their behavior might best be described not as progress or the lack of it toward a professional ideal that incorporated ethical considerations, but as activities sanctioned or not by a CoP. In the late nineteenth century, reporters and editors were struggling to fill larger newspapers made possible and profitable by a torrent of new technologies and advertising. They existed in a highly competitive environment that required them to quickly master the basics of newswork. CoPs, with their informal structures and shared concerns, appear to have been an efficient way to master these skills. To survive in the process, journalists developed a parallel system of work rules governing delinquent behavior. These "rule-breaking" conventions punished abusive superiors by sabotaging story assignments, equalized workloads through combination reporting arrangements, and pursued personal advancement by "staging" or "faking" stories. Delinquency codes also conflicted with a reporter's duty to produce accurate, routine stories as well as exclusives or scoops. Cubs probably learned how to be delinquents in the same manner and from the same sources that taught them the accepted standards of journalism. For the nineteenth-century reporter, rule-breaking was not extraordinary behavior. It was common; it was freely discussed; it was not reported to superiors. Some dailies, like the *Boston Globe*, seemed to exist only to manufacture gargantuan "fakes." Kelly, who admitted to generating her own fakes and who described how a co-worker had produced a fake about a volcanic eruption in the South Pacific, also described in her work autobiography how a *Globe* exchange editor had invented a Massachusetts town. Kelly wrote that the editor, a Harvard graduate, explained how he had solved the problem of exchange stories without datelines that he wished to use. He invented a newspaper for a faraway New England town too small to have its own weekly or daily. Thereafter, stories with a questionable provenance were assigned as originating at the imaginary newspaper.[5]

Besides survival and convenience, there may have been a second compelling reason for developing and applying rule-breaking standards: Cubs and other news workers perceived succeeding in journalism to be a test of character and believed that their personal code of ethics would prove a superior guide in this effort. Gilded Age Americans pursued many activities that would "build" character, from the Boy Scouts to adult education programs. The influence and ubiquity of these efforts permeated society.[6] They received the blessings of publications like *Scientific American*, whose contributors wrote of the national character: "We have a passion for improvement, not merely in our mechanical industries but in our social life and in our municipal and national governments."[7] The generation born at mid-century keenly felt the need for achievement and self-improvement.[8] Their fathers' generation had distinguished itself both in war and peace and now feared young men moving to large cities would fall victim to poker, prostitutes, and sensational publications once the stabilizing forces of family, church, and community were removed.[9] Their character—defined by a Harvard professor as how far a person would reach for their ideals—was just now being tested.[10] If need be, they would fudge newswork rules enough to pass the character test.

The tests for cub reporters who wrote occupational memoirs or their colleagues who wrote fictions could be both physical and mental. Richard Harding Davis's Gallegher and Baker's Pippins endured snow and physical danger to secure scoops; Munroe's Myles Manning flirted with gambling and drinking addictions that nearly cost him his career. The newsboys in James Otis Kaler's juvenile novel overcame setbacks from a fire and a false arrest.

In reality, Lincoln Steffens would not accept bribes from investors while covering the bank panic of 1893, but he did not consider it an ethical blunder to speculate privately in the stock market at the same time. Ethics, he wrote, were radically different for the businessman and the politician, who came from different cultures. The differences were so great "that a business man in politics will commit sins appalling to the politician, and vice versa. Morals are matters of trade or profession and form the ethics they are supposed to be formed by."[11]

In the more than one hundred years since Koenigsberg began compiling his standards for newswork, much has changed, but there are strong parallels between then and now. CoPs appear to still function as an alternative source of instruction for journalists, "fakes" continue to be a part of the news landscape, and technological developments are reshaping how stories are narrated and edited much as the new technologies changed newswork in the 1880s. The present economy also can be volatile.

City room ethnographies conducted by academics with more rigorous training than that of the "academic muckrakers" of the late nineteenth century have found some of the parallels between now and then. In some cases, those parallels seem to be constants. For example, reporters studied at the mid-point of the twentieth century apparently still learned how to recognize and handle a "policy" or "sacred cow" story in the same way as their nineteenth-century counterparts.[12] Novices were not told which policy stories required a positive or negative slant; they learned it by imitating how other reporters wrote those stories or by observing how their stories were edited. Twentieth-century cubs learned those routines over months or years and were not considered veteran or star reporters until they could be depended upon to write stories sympathetic to their newspaper's policy orientation. Some policy considerations were so ingrained that they transcended any single news organization and reflected national-level values, as sociologist Herbert J. Gans found in his ethnographic work with network news and news magazines. These Gansian "enduring values" included ethnocentrism, altruistic democracy, responsible capitalism, small-town pastoralism, individualism, moderatism, social order, and national leadership.[13] British sociologist Brian McNair made a similar point. Journalism "is essentially ideological—a communicative vehicle for the transmission to an audience (intentionally or otherwise) not just of facts but of the assumptions, attitudes, beliefs and values of its maker(s), drawn from and expressive of a particular world-view."[14] These values are so entrenched that reporters and producers unconsciously "frame" stories with them in much the same way as nineteenth-century practitioners built their stories around the elements of Joseph Pulitzer's "new journalism" or Charles Dana's "human interest" reporting.[15]

Journalists from both centuries also shared similar ideas about when rule-breaking was an acceptable act of delinquency. Mark Fishman's study of the press corps in a mid-size California town found that reporters from a variety of media, not just newspapers, used a form of combination reporting that nineteenth-century reporters would have recognized.[16] This sharing of information among members of the combine matched the "common property" exchanges among nineteenth-century reporters described by *New York Sun* editor Edward P. Mitchell.[17] If a reporter was late to cover an event, the California journalists would share the information he or she missed. Incidental information like the spelling of names, identification of people attending a meeting, or clarification of a bureaucratic process also would be shared. Unreported gossip about sources also was considered communal property. In addition, reporters would update each other about when an event with news value would occur. Other media researchers have observed the same sharing by reporters, noting that it not only involved competitors from other news organizations, but a reporter's competitors within the same organization.[18]

A consensus also had developed in the California market about what would not be shared: Specific tips on news stories, details about news events that a reporter had not covered but now sought information about, and the identity of sources were not shared. The press corps tolerated the occasional "scoop" or exclusive story by one of its members, "with no hard feelings expected or permissible."[19] The reasons why these exceptions were granted were similar to those cited by California reporters a hundred years earlier.[20] As an apprentice for seven months on one of the newspapers, Fishman realized that he was learning newswork from observing more experienced reporters, much like the experiences of cub reporters in the nineteenth century. Fishman wrote:

> [M]y apprenticeship field notes reflected how I learned to pay attention to things happening at meetings. I learned when to take breaks and time-outs from long sessions by noticing what other reporters were and were not paying attention to. Most importantly, I discovered why certain occurrences were not of interest and, thus, why they became invisible to reporters.[21]

A similar study of the media in Philadelphia found that reporters still relied almost exclusively on the interview, the chief news-gathering tool of the late nineteenth century, rather than on documents or official reports. The interview had become what sociologist Phyllis Kaniss called one of journalism's "standard operating procedures."[22] Or, as Fishman wrote in his evaluation of sources and news: "Something is so because somebody says it."[23] Once collected from a source interview, facts had to be turned into a narrative. Older reporters in Gaye Tuchman's ethnographic study learned how to write stories as they served a newsroom apprenticeship that might require years to complete. They mastered basic story structures, but they also learned when to break format rules. Tuchman observed: "Professionalism may mean breaking those rules that serve as bibles for hacks."[24] Some Gilded Age reporters, like Irvin Cobb, reached the same conclusion in their work memoirs.[25]

Since the advent of the twenty-first century, new digital media also have altered how fast and how well stories are written and edited. The new media technologies have moved society from "information scarcity and tight distribution to information abundance and media fragmentation."[26] Scoops have become rarer, but the opportunity to provide context for a story has increased.[27] As in the Gilded Age, the changes have come at a cost. The accelerated news cycle, reductions in editing staffs, and multi-tasking on several platforms have produced what some media critics refer to as the "Era of Error."[28] The digital pathways also have made it possible for the creators of fake news to spread their messages.[29]

News workers also have changed. Most "digital age" reporters have bachelor's degrees, but only about half of U.S. journalists with a college degree majored in journalism or communication.[30] Instead, media companies are likely to pursue job candidates with degrees in computer or data sciences. Those degrees are expected to help cubs master multiple, digital platforms in today's convergent city rooms or to prepare them to serve as knowledge brokers for co-workers.[31] These "digital" employees, however, may not be familiar with the basic rules of newswork. About 60 percent of the journalists responding to a recent survey believed their occupation was headed in the wrong direction. "Hasty reporting," threats from online media, and a shrinking labor force troubled them.[32] Survey respondents also feared they were losing the autonomy to select their own stories.[33] They rejected using confidential business or government documents without authorization, using personal documents like letters and photographs without permission, badgering unwilling sources, securing employment to get insider information, and other unwholesome tactics to obtain stories. Not all nineteenth-century reporters would have rejected those same procedures.

Not only can the CoP model be helpful in decoding the flow of information through nineteenth-century journalism, it could prove useful in understanding the circulation of the same information during the present period of "retrenchment and reappraisal."[34] In the past seventeen years, scholarly and general interest in CoPs as a model for understanding the spread and management of new knowledge has gained traction. A recent check of a database of communication journals found "Community" or "Communities of Practice" used in the title of fifty-six studies. None was published before 1997.[35] In these essays and research projects, CoP concepts were used to understand how present-day journalists adjust their professional norms and practices to fit new social media technologies,[36] to manage the convergence of these technologies in newsrooms,[37] to shape new methods of communication,[38] and to understand past news worker behavior. The parallels between newsroom knowledge management in the late nineteenth century and today also may offer us a way to anticipate even more distant developments in newswork.

# Notes

## Preface

1. The bibliographic essay in Ted Curtis Smythe, *The Gilded Age Press,* is an excellent guide to the literature. Fred Fedler, *Lessons from the Past: Journalists' Lives and Work, 1850–1950* is a good presentation of the primary source material.

## Chapter One. Introduction

1. Moses Koenigsberg, *King News: An Autobiography,* 98.
2. Scott Derks, *The Middle Class,* vol. 2 of *Working Americans 1880–1999,* 1.
3. Yochanan Shachmurove, "A Historical Overview of Financial Crisis in the United States," 217–31.
4. Derks, *The Middle Class,* 1.
5. John O'Sullivan and Edward F. Keuchel, *American Economic History: From Abundance to Constraint,* 95–121.
6. Scott Derks, *The Working Class,* vol. 1 of *Working Americans 1880–1999,* 2.
7. O'Sullivan and Keuchel, *American Economic History,* 95–121.
8. Williams S. Rossiter, "Special Reports on Selected Industries, Printing and Publishing," *12th Census of the United States—Manufactures, Part III,* 1039.
9. A. F., "The Linotype and the Man Who Made It," 2–3.
10. Incredible typesetting speeds were possible with Mergenthaler's linotype. A *New York Tribune* operator using a linotype set 411,200 ems of type in forty-eight hours and five minutes in 1894. See "A Record Broken," 1. An em is as wide and as high as the type point size being set. Linotype operators could produce from 3,600 to 6,000 ems per hour. By the fall of 1894, about 1,000 linotypes were in use by 150 U.S. newspapers and book publishers. See "Linotype," 8.
11. "Christmas Journal Chief Triumph of Printing Art," 58.
12. Rossiter, "Printing and Publishing," 1087.
13. Arthur Robb, "Modern Presses Began in Eighties," sec. 2, 198.
14. Rossiter, "Printing and Publishing," 1087.

15. Rossiter identified the relevant technologies as machine composition, perfecting presses, line cut and half-tone illustrations, cheap, but high quality paper made from wood-pulp, and plate-making advances. See Rossiter, "Printing and Publishing," 1086–1105.

16. "The Editor's Assistant," 6.

17. Rossiter, "Printing and Publishing," 1044. Publishing industry statistics collected for the census in 1880, 1890, and 1900 cannot always be compared with confidence. The 1880 census, for instance, did not use uniform schedules of inquiry for all publishers. The 1880 and 1890 censuses also treated statistics differently for book and job printing. In 1880, book and job-related statistics for companies that published newspapers and periodicals were excluded. In 1890, the same numbers were included. The 1900 census attempted to treat book and job printing—no matter where it was done—as a separate statistical entity.

18. Ibid., 1090.

19. Ibid., Table 7, 1048.

20. All three censuses estimated periodical failure rates the same way. They assumed that periodicals that did not complete the census forms had stopped publishing or were too small to affect the reported statistical conclusions.

21. Rossiter, "Printing and Publishing," Table 19, 1047.

22. Ted Curtis Smythe, *The Gilded Age Press, 1865–1900*, 149–71; Marion Tuttle Marzolf, *Civilizing Voices: American Press Criticism 1880–1950*, 7–8.

23. Marianne Salcetti, "The Emergence of the Reporter: Mechanization and the Devaluation of Editorial Workers," in *News Workers: Toward a History of the Rank and File*, ed. Hanno Hardt and Bonnie Brennen, 48–74.

24. Rossiter, "Printing and Publishing," 1089.

25. Ibid.

26. Census takers in 1880, 1890, and 1900 reported publishing employees as salaried officials and clerks or wage earners, the category which included reporters and editors as well as the technicians who operated the new press technologies. The 1880 and 1890 censuses tried to provide reporter, editor, and subeditor breakdowns for the wage earner category; Rossiter did not attempt to make the same distinction in 1900. The mechanical technicians, however, controlled the new press technologies, making them less expendable.

27. Rossiter, "Printing and Publishing," Table 5, 1042.

28. Haryot Holt Cahoon, "Women in Gutter Journalism," 568–74; "Women in Newspaper Work," 9.

29. Margaret E. Sangster, "Editorship as a Profession for Women," 445–55.

30. Elizabeth G. Jordan, "The Newspaper Woman's Story [Journalist Series]," 340–47.

31. Jeannette L. Gilder, "Journalism for Girls," 656A.

32. Elizabeth G. Jordan, "What It Means to Be a Newspaper Woman," 8.

33. Jean Marie Lutes, *Front-Page Girls: Women Journalists in American Culture and Fiction, 1880–1930.*

34. Patricia Bradley, *Women and the Press: The Struggle for Equality.*

35. Jessie M. Wood, "The Newspaper Woman," 372.

36. Lutes, *Front-Page Girls*, 13.

37. Stunt girls have been rehabilitated as representing a pathway to legitimate newswork. See Brooke Kroeger, *Nellie Bly: Daredevil, Reporter, Feminist*; Randall S. Sumpter, "'Girl Reporter': Elizabeth L. Banks and the 'Stunt' Genre," 60–77.

38. Montgomery-M'Govern, "An Important Phase," 240–53; Cahoon, "Women in Gutter Journalism," 568–74.

39. Rheta Childe Dorr, *A Woman of Fifty*, 75.

40. S. N. D. North, "History and Present Condition of the Newspaper and Periodical Press of the United States," *10*$^{th}$ *Census of the United States*, 58–59.

41. Ibid., 83.

42. Ibid., 93.

43. Ibid., 73.

44. Rossiter, "Printing and Publishing," 1046.

45. Ibid., 1042; "A Primer of Journalism," 8.

46. Kirk Munroe, *Under Orders: The Story of a Young Reporter*, 15.

47. Isaac F. Marcosson, *Adventures in Interviewing*, 17. The anecdotes reported here are drawn from each man's autobiography.

48. Jessica Isaac, "Youthful Enterprises: Amateur Newspapers and the Pre-History of Adolescence, 1867–1883," 158–77.

49. Depending upon the version, the press could cost from fifteen to fifty dollars. See Paula Petrik, "The Youngest Fourth Estate: The Novelty Toy Printing Press and Adolescence, 1870–1886," 127.

50. For instance, John M. Jones marketed the Star Printing Press from offices in New York, Chicago, Boston, and Philadelphia. His hobby press came in four sizes and sold for sixty, thirty-eight, twenty-five, or twelve dollars. See Frank Cropper, *The Amateur Journalists' Companion.*

51. Isaac, "Youthful Enterprises," 160.

52. Cropper, *Amateur Journalists' Companion*, 17.

53. "Playing with the Pen," *Washington Post*, March 9, 1896, 4. Isaac, "Youthful Enterprises," 163; Robert H. Woodward, *Jack London and the Amateur Press*; Truman Joseph Spencer, *The History of Amateur Journalism*, 11.

54. John Travis Nixon, comp., "Explanatory," to *A History of the National Amateur Press Association.*

55. "Employment for Boys," 369.

56. H. Prince, "Our Young Contributors: How Harry Got His Printing-Press," 368–71.

57. Sara Lindey, "Boys Write Back: Self-Education and Periodical Authorship in Late-Nineteenth-Century Story Papers," 73.

58. William Salisbury, *The Career of a Journalist*, 2.

59. Ibid., 518.

60. Dorr, *A Woman of Fifty*, 68.

61. "The Making of a Newspaper," 11.

62. Samuel G. Blythe, *The Making of a Newspaper Man*.

63. Florence Finch Kelly, *Flowing Stream: The Story of Fifty-Six Years in American Newspaper Life*, 145.

64. Elizabeth L. Banks, *The Autobiography of a "Newspaper Girl."*

65. Charles Edward Russell, *These Shifting Scenes,* 38.

66. J. Lincoln Steffens, "VI. The Business of a Newspaper (The Conduct of Great Businesses—Sixth Paper)," 447–67.

67. Ibid., 458.

## Chapter Two. The Theoreticians

1. Jane Thomas, "Business Writing in History: What Caused the Dictamen's Demise?" 40–54.

2. Michael Burger, "Notes and Documents: The Date and Authorship of Robert Grosseteste's Rules for Household and Estate Management," 106–16.

3. Roy A. Atwood and Arnold S. de Beer, "The Roots of Academic News Research: Tobias Peucer's 'De relationibus Novellis (1690),'" 485–96.

4. Ibid., 492.

5. Ibid., 488–89.

6. Randall S. Sumpter, "News About News: Speed and the First Quantitative Newspaper Content Analysis," 64–72. They were called the "academic muckrakers" because their work carried over into the Progressive Era and because it was fundamentally a critique of new journalism.

7. See Klaus Krippendorff, *Content Analysis: An Introduction to Its Methodology*, 15–16; Bernard Berelson, *Content Analysis in Communication Research*, 206; and Frances Fenton, "The Influence of Newspaper Presentations Upon the Growth of Crime and Other Anti-Social Activity," 342–71. Fenton's two-part study continues under the same title in the *American Journal of Sociology's* January 1911 issue. Speed's work is the earliest newspaper study cited by Berelson and Fenton. See John Gilmer Speed, "Do Newspapers Now Give the News?" 705–11.

8. His mother, Emma Keats, was poet John Keats's niece. His father, Philip, served as a major in the U.S. Army and as collector of internal revenue for

Kentucky during the Civil War. An uncle, James Speed, served as attorney general in Abraham Lincoln's cabinet. A second uncle, Joshua, was a Louisville merchant, newspaper editor, and Lincoln acquaintance. The details of Speed's life can be found in *Who Was Who in America, 1897–1942*, vol. 1, 1160–61; *The National Cyclopaedia of American Biography*, vol. 10, 294–95; and James Grant Wilson and John Fiske, eds., *Appletons' Cyclopaedia of American Biography*, vol. 5, 625–26.

9. C. R. Miller, "A Word to the Critics of Newspapers," 712–17.

10. J. W. Keller, "Journalism as a Career," 691–704.

11. The *World* had the biggest page gain, growing from eight pages in a seven-column format to forty-four pages in an eight-column format. The *Times* showed the lowest growth rate, from sixteen pages to twenty pages. The *Tribune* doubled its twelve-page 1881 size; the *Sun* grew from eight to twenty-eight pages.

12. These and other declines generally were percentage decreases on initially small column totals.

13. Speed, "Do Newspapers Now Give the News?" 711.

14. The author reviewed the editorial pages of the *Sun*, *World*, *Tribune*, and *Times* published between August 1, 1893, and September 30, 1893. Before publication of the August *Forum*, the *Times* ran a short notice on its editorial page about the issue that noted the contributions, including Speed's, about the newspaper business. See "The 'Forum' for August," 4.

15. "A Newspaper Symposium," 79–81.

16. "Journalism as a Profession," 12–13.

17. Besides Fenton's two-part study, the others were: Delos F. Wilcox, "The American Newspaper: A Study in Social Psychology," 56–92; Byron C. Mathews, "A Study of a New York Daily," 82–86; James Edwards Rogers, *The American Newspaper*; Arthur I. Street, "The Truth About the Newspaper. A Remarkable Summary, by Arthur I. Street of American Publications, Proving that Crime and Sensationalism Occupy a Comparatively Small Space in the Volume of the Day's News," sec. G, 2; Alvan A. Tenney, "The Scientific Analysis of the Press," 276–77.

18. Wilcox, "The American Newspaper," 56–92.

19. Tenney, "Scientific Analysis," 896.

20. Stanley J. Baran and Dennis K. Davis, *Mass Communication Theory: Foundations, Ferment, and Future*, 7th ed., 46–47.

21. Robert E. Park, "The Natural History of the Newspaper," 276.

22. Robert E. Park, "Reflections on Communication and Culture," 204.

23. Robert E. Park, "The Yellow Press," 3–11.

24. P. J. Frazier and Cecilie Gaziano, "Robert Ezra Park's Theory of News, Public Opinion and Social Control"; Stephen D. Reese and Jane Ballinger, "The

Roots of a Sociology of News: Remembering Mr. Gates and Social Control in the Newsroom," 641–58.

25. D. Charles Whitney, Randall S. Sumpter, and Denis McQuail, "News Media Production: Individuals, Organizations, Institutions," 393–410. Allport, a Harvard social psychologist, and his research associate coded more than 1,500 newspaper stories, editorials, letters to the editor, and columns about a foreign policy issue. They also used Gallup poll data. The two looked for examples of "news coloring" where they believed the personal views of news workers had slipped into the text. White, Prugger, and Swanson designed studies with more direct methods of gauging news worker background and its effect on news writing or selection. White, for instance, interviewed a wire editor about why he used some stories and rejected others.

26. Gaye Tuchman, *Making News: A Study in the Construction of Reality.*

27. Mark Fishman, *Manufacturing the News.*

28. Phyllis C. Kaniss, *Making Local News.*

29. Everett M. Rogers, *Diffusion of Innovations*, 5th ed., 40–42.

30. Gabriel Tarde, *Gabriel Tarde on Communication and Social Influence: Selected Papers,* ed. Terry N. Clark, 21.

31. Ibid., 31.

32. Rogers, *Diffusion of Innovations*, 40–43.

33. Ibid., 12.

34. Melvin L. DeFleur, *Mass Communication Theories: Explaining Origins, Processes, and Effects*, 277–79.

35. Andrew H. Van de Ven et al., *The Innovation Journey*, 16.

36. John Dimmick, "Sex, Violence, and the Rules of the Game: Canons and Codes as Occupational Ideologies," 182.

37. Horst Pöttker, "News and Its Communicative Quality: The Inverted Pyramid—When and Why Did It Appear," 510.

38. Michael Schudson, "The Politics of Narrative Form: The Emergence of News Conventions in Print and Television," 100.

39. Ted Curtis Smythe, "The Diffusion of the Urban Daily, 1850–1900," 73–84.

40. Bert N. Adams and R. A. Sydie, *Sociological Theory*, 384–85.

41. Andrew Cox, "What Are Communities of Practice? A Comparative Review of Four Seminal Works," 527–40.

42. Etienne Wenger, "Communities of Practice and Social Learning Systems," 229.

43. Etienne Wenger, *Communities of Practice: Learning, Meaning, and Identity*; Amy Schmitz Weiss and David Domingo, "Innovation Processes in Online Newsrooms as Actor-Networks and Communities of Practice," 1156–71;

Elisabeth Davenport and Hazel Hall, "Organisational Knowledge and Communities of Practice," 171–227.

44. Wenger, *Communities of Practice*, 83.

45. Harry Scarbrough and Jacky Swan, "Knowledge Communities and Innovation," 7–18; Heather A. Smith and James D. McKeen, "Creating and Facilitating Communities of Practice" in *Handbook of Knowledge Management 1: Knowledge Matters*, ed. C. W. Holsapple, 393–407; J. David Johnson, "Influence Relationships Within a Community of Practice," 63–92.

46. Johnson, "Influence Relationships," 63–92.

47. Wenger, *Communities of Practice*, 127.

48. Wenger, "Communities of Practice," 225–46; Scarbrough and Swan, "Knowledge Communities," 7–18.

49. Wenger, "Communities of Practice," 225–46.

50. Davenport and Hall, "Organizational Knowledge," 200.

51. Wenger, "Communities of Practice," 225–46.

52. The 150 total is known as Dunbar's Number, named for the British anthropologist. See Robin Dunbar, *How Many Friends Does One Person Need? Dunbar's Number and Other Evolutionary Quirks*.

53. Smith and McKeen, "Creating and Facilitating," 393–407.

54. Examples include: Stephen A. Banning, "The Professionalization of Journalism: A Nineteenth-Century Beginning," 157–63; Ronald R. Rodgers, "Journalism Is a Loose-Jointed Thing: A Content Analysis of *Editor & Publisher*'s Discussion of Journalistic Conduct Prior to the Canons of Journalism, 1901–1922," 66–82; Mary M. Cronin, "Trade Press Roles in Promoting Journalistic Professionalism, 1884–1917," *Journal of Mass Media Ethics* 8, no. 4 (1993): 227–38; Patrick Lee Plaisance, "A Gang of Pecksniffs Grows Up: The Evolution of Journalism Ethics Discourse in *The Journalist* and *Editor and Publisher*," 479–91; Joseph A. Mirando, "Embracing Objectivity Early On: Journalism Textbooks of the 1800s," 23–32.

55. Hazel Dicken-Garcia, *Journalistic Standards in Nineteenth-Century America*, 10.

56. Ibid., 11.

57. Plaisance, "A Gang of Pecksniffs," 482.

58. Patricia L. Dooley, *The Technology of Journalism: Cultural Agents, Cultural Icons*, 54–55.

59. Allan Forman, introduction to "The Blue Pencil and How to Avoid It," by Alex G. Nevins, 12.

60. David A. Curtis, "Tips for the Boys," 7.

61. Irvin S. Cobb, *Exit Laughing*, 134.

62. Charles Edward Russell, *These Shifting Scenes*, 301.

63. Robert Luce, *Writing for the Press: A Manual for Editors, Reporters, Correspondents, and Printers*, 4th ed., rev., 71.

64. E. L. Shuman, *Steps Into Journalism: Helps and Hints for Young Writers*, 26.

65. Ibid., 23.

66. By An Editor [pseud.], preface to *Hints to Young Editors.*

67. J. G. Schuman, "Teaching—A Trade or a Profession?" 171–85; Lewis Meriam, "The Trend Toward Professionalization," 58–64.

68. Edward T. Silva and Sheila Slaughter, "Prometheus Bound: The Limits of Social Science Professionalization in the Progressive Period," 781–819.

69. Burton J. Bledstein, *The Culture of Professionalism: The Middle Class and the Development of Higher Education in America*, 100.

70. Ibid., 101. As used here, "New Journalism" generally refers to the innovations and sensational content introduced by Joseph Pulitzer and his contemporaries, not the literary style of writing practiced during the 1960s and 1970s that is also known as "New Journalism."

71. William J. Goode, "Community Within a Community: The Professions," 194–200.

72. Lawrence Klatt, "The Professionalization of Everyone," 508–09, 522.

73. Andrew Delano Abbott, *The System of Professions: An Essay on the Division of Expert Labor.*

74. Ibid., 215.

75. Patricia L. Dooley, *Taking Their Political Place: Journalists and the Making of an Occupation.*

76. William F. May, "Professional Ethics, the University, and the Journalist," 20–31. Proprietary for-profit schools are not included in the percentages.

77. Katherine H. Adams, *A History of Professional Writing Instruction in American Colleges: Years of Acceptance, Growth, and Doubt*, 100.

78. Linda Steiner, "Construction of Gender in Newsreporting Textbooks: 1890–1990," 5; Christopher Wilson, *The Labor of Words: Literary Professionalism in the Progressive Era*, 20–24.

79. For example, German women who sought apprenticeships in nursing had to care for a terminally ill patient first. See Karen Nolte, "'Telling the Painful Truth'—Nurses and Physicians in the Nineteenth Century," 115–34.

80. De Forest O'Dell, *The History of Journalism Education in the United States*, 40, 45.

81. M. Lyle Spencer, *News Writing: The Gathering, Handling and Writing of News Stories*, viii.

82. Walter Avenel, "Journalism as a Profession," 366–74; James Parton, "Journalism as a Profession for Young Men," 103–6.

83. E. L. Shuman, *Steps Into Journalism: Helps and Hints for Young Writers*, Preface.

84. Keller, "Journalism as a Career," 699.

85. "A Professorship of Journalism," 2.

86. Henri de Blowitz, "The Profession. There Are Others, But They Are Not 'In It,'" 8.

87. G. A. Gaskell, *How to Write for the Press*, 17.

88. Elizabeth L. Banks, *The Autobiography of a "Newspaper Girl"*, 311.

89. Shuman, *Steps Into Journalism*, x.

90. The definition of trade journal used here is among the shorter ones found in the literature. See Roland B. Smith, "The Genesis of the Business Press in the United States," 146.

91. Julien Elfenbein, *Business Journalism*, 2nd rev. ed., 14–15.

92. "Get News of Trade," 4.

93. "Trade Press Association," 9.

94. "Editorial Policy of Trade Press," 3.

95. While not the first trade journal for the press, *The Journalist* was the most useful, according to Smythe. For more details about the period trade press, see the bibliographical essay in Ted Curtis Smythe, *The Gilded Age Press, 1865–1900*, 217–20.

96. The target audience evaluations in this paragraph are from Mott. See Frank Luther Mott, *A History of American Magazines, Vol. IV: 1885–1905*, 243–44.

97. Cronin, "Trade Press Roles," 227–38.

98. Kenneth T. Andrews and Neal Caren, "Making the News: Movement Organizations, Media Attention, and the Public Agenda," 841–66.

99. David Michael Ryfe, "The Nature of News Rules," 203.

100. Sarah Sobieraj, "Reporting Conventions: Journalists, Activists and the Thorny Struggle for Political Visibility," 505–28.

101. Markus C. Becker, "Organizational Routines: A Review of the Literature," 643–77.

102. Elizabeth A. Hoffman, "'Revenge' and 'Rescue': Workplace Deviance in the Taxicab Industry," 270.

103. D. E. Chubin, "Research Malpractice," 80–89.

104. Ted Curtis Smythe, "The Reporter, 1880–1900. Working Conditions and Their Influence on the News," 8.

105. Plaisance, "A Gang of Pecksniffs Grows Up," 481.

106. Howard Good, *The Journalist as Autobiographer*; Susan Balée, "From the Outside in: A History of American Autobiography," 40–64; Fred Fedler, "Actions of Early Journalists Often Unethical, Even Illegal," 160–70.

107. Jeremy D. Popkin, *History, Historians, & Autobiography*; Linda Steiner, "Sex, Lives, and Autobiography: Contributions of Life Study to Journalism History: What Can Be Learned," 206–11.

108. Good, *Journalist as Autobiographer*, 10.

109. Alexander Lee, "Portrait of the Author as a Historian," 54–55.

110. Michael I. Carignan, "Fiction as History or History as Fiction? George Eliot, Hayden White, and Nineteenth-Century Historicism," 395–415.

## Chapter Three. The News Debate

1. Mary M. Cronin, "Trade Press Roles in Promoting Journalistic Professionalism, 1884–1917," 227–38.

2. Rheta Childe Dorr, *A Woman of Fifty*, 74.

3. Moses Koenigsberg, *King News: An Autobiography*, 13.

4. William Salisbury, *The Career of a Journalist*, 518.

5. Isaac F. Marcosson, *Adventures in Interviewing*, 38–39.

6. Julian Ralph, *The Making of a Journalist*, 138.

7. Ray Stannard Baker, *American Chronicle: The Autobiography of Ray Stannard Baker*, 93.

8. Will Irwin, *The Making of a Reporter*, 125.

9. Salisbury, *Career of a Journalist*, 17.

10. William J. Goode, "Community Within a Community: The Professions," 194–200; Lawrence Klatt, "The Professionalization of Everyone," 508–9, 522; William F. May, "Professional Ethics, The University, and The Journalist," 20–31.

11. Mark Canada, ed., *Literature and Journalism: Inspirations, Intersections, and Inventions from Ben Franklin to Stephen Colbert*.

12. Christopher P. Wilson, *The Labor of Words: Literary Professionalism in the Progressive Era*, 201.

13. Mitchell Stephens, *A History of News*, 3rd ed., 4.

14. Canada, *Literature and Journalism*, 2.

15. E. L. Shuman, *Steps Into Journalism: Helps and Hints for Young Writers*, 192.

16. Catherine Mitchell, "Greeley as journalism teacher: 'give us facts, occurrences,'" 16–19.

17. Ibid., 18.

18. William E. Huntzicker, *The Popular Press, 1833–1865*, 170.

19. Baker, *American Chronicle*, 11. Aside from the "fact, not opinion" rule, his additional guidelines were: Do not use a notebook, it might unsettle a source; do not overwrite; do report common human suffering and common human joy; do ensure your stories are "interesting, interesting, interesting."

20. Kent Cooper, *Kent Cooper and the Associated Press*, 195.

21. Jesse Lynch Williams, *The Stolen Story and Other Newspaper Stories*, 247.

22. Lincoln Steffens, *The Autobiography of Lincoln Steffens: Complete in One Volume*.

23. John Palmer Gavit, "What Is News? A Manual for Newspaper Reporters and Correspondents," 12–13.

24. Samuel Hopkins Adams, *The Clarion*, 99; T. J. Norton, "News, and How to Get It," 279.

25. John Palmer Gavit, "What Is News? Sources of News, Tricks of the Trade, and Hints on Ways and Means," 10.

26. Ibid., 14.

27. James Luby, *James Luby: Journalist*, 18.

28. Edward Arden, "The Evolution of the Newspaper," 152–54; Seyon [pseud.], "News-Gathering in Washington: The Special Correspondent," 452–54; Shuman, *Steps Into Journalism.*

29. Seyon, "News-Gathering in Washington," 452.

30. Shuman, *Steps Into Journalism*, 11.

31. William Harlan Hale, *Horace Greeley: Voice of the People*, 68.

32. "What Is News—Should the People Get It All?" 130.

33. "The Future of Newspapers," 152.

34. Irvin S. Cobb, *Exit Laughing*, 119.

35. Shuman, *Steps Into Journalism*, 98–99.

36. William P. Trent, *The Authority of Criticism and Other Essays*, 147.

37. W. H. Crawshaw, *The Interpretation of Literature*, 3.

38. Adams Sherman Hill, *Our English*, 139.

39. Norman Hapgood, "American Art Criticism," 45–47.

40. Hill, *Our English*, 120, 125–26.

41. "Journalism and Literature," 4.

42. Hill, *Our English*, 128.

43. Ibid., 107.

44. Archie Emerson Palmer, "Some Experiences in a Newspaper Office," 29–30.

45. Ibid., 29.

46. "Newspaper English," 14.

47. Franklin Matthews, "Newspaper English," 302–5.

48. Gavit, "Sources of News," 12.

49. Alex G. Nevins, "The Blue Pencil and How to Avoid It," April 26, 1890, 13.

50. Alex G. Nevins, "The Blue Pencil and How to Avoid It," May 3, 1890, 12.

51. Robert Luce, *Writing for the Press: A Manual for Editors, Reporters, Correspondents, and Printers*, 50.

52. "Some Newspaper English," 866.

53. Luce, *Writing for the Press*, 46.

54. Shuman, *Steps Into Journalism*, 60.

55. T. Campbell-Copeland, "Ladder of Journalism: How to Climb It," 13; "Making a Journalist," 1, 6; C. W. Willis, "Newspaper Correspondence.

Practical Hints and Rules by a Working Correspondent," 44; E. M. C. French, "Study Your Paper," 30.

56. Kirk Munroe, *Under Orders: The Story of a Young Reporter.*

57. Shuman, *Steps Into Journalism*, 94.

58. M. L. Rayne, *What Can a Woman Do: Her Position in the Business and Literary World*, 41.

59. Randall S. Sumpter, "Learning the 'Outsider' Profession: Serial Advice Columns in *The Journalist*," 9.

60. One of the Brotherhood [pseud.], "The Literary Aspirant," 997.

61. Munroe, *Under Orders*, 253.

62. Augustus Thomas, *The Print of My Remembrance*, 191.

63. An Every Day Scribbler [pseud.], "The Scribbler and His Paymaster," 1840.

64. W. D. Howells, "Authors and Authorship: The Man of Letters as a Man of Business," 437.

65. Ibid., 437.

66. Ibid., 429–45.

67. Charles Johanningsmeier, *Fiction and the American Literary Marketplace: The Role of Newspaper Syndicates, 1860–1900*; Alexis Weedon, *Victorian Publishing: The Economics of Book Production for a Mass Market, 1836–1916.*

## Chapter Four. The Rule Writers

1. "Writing for the Press," 10.

2. James Parton, "Journalism as a Profession for Young Men," 103–6.

3. Frank Luther Mott, *A History of American Magazines*, vol. 4, 514.

4. John H. Vincent, *The Chautauqua Movement with an introduction by President Lewis Miller*, 206.

5. While not the first trade journal for the press, *The Journalist* was the most useful, according to Smythe. For more details about the period trade press, see the bibliographical essay in Ted Curtis Smythe, *The Gilded Age Press, 1865–1900*, 217–20.

6. Based on self-reports to *N. W. Ayer & Son's American Newspaper Annual*, 354. After competitors appeared in the 1890s, *The Journalist*'s circulation fluctuated between 5,000 and 6,000 copies a week. See *N. W. Ayer & Son's American Newspaper Annual* (1890), 508; *N. W. Ayer & Son's American Newspaper Annual* (1894), 542. Forman claimed the first issue of *The Journalist* sold 5,000 copies, the entire press run. See "A Very Great Success," 6.

7. H. L. Mencken, *Newspaper Days: 1899–1906*, 12.

8. James Stanford Bradshaw, "Mrs. Rayne's School of Journalism," 513–17, 579.

9. Alta Halverson Seymour, "What Can a Woman Do," 6; Norma H. Goodhue, "Always Look Ahead, Educator Tells Women," C2.

10. Bradshaw, *Mrs. Rayne's School of Journalism*, 517; Albert Nelson Marquis, ed., *Who's Who in America: A Biographical Dictionary of Notable Living Men and Women of the United States*, vol. 1910–1911., 1577.

11. Irvin S. Cobb, *Exit Laughing*, 142.

12. Fred Fedler, *Lessons from the Past: Journalists' Lives and Work, 1850–1950*, 231–34.

13. Edward Page Mitchell, *Memoirs of an Editor: Fifty Years of American Journalism*, 79.

14. Julian Ralph, *The Making of a Journalist*, 57.

15. Kirk Munroe, *Under Orders: The Story of a Young Reporter*, 84, 347.

16. Shuman, *Steps Into Journalism*, 124.

17. Elizabeth Garver Jordan, *Tales of the City Room.*

18. Ibid., 96.

19. Shuman, *Steps Into Journalism*, 103.

20. "Making a Journalist," 1, 6.

21. "College Journalism," 4.

22. Henri de Blowitz, "The Profession. There Are Others, But They Are Not 'In It,'" 8.

23. Foster Coates, "Paying City Journalism," 12; "Chairs of Journalism," 4; "Schools of Journalism," 8.

24. "The Country Newspaper," 5; Editor of the Journalist [pseud.], "One of Many," 6; Thomas Campbell-Copeland, "The Ladder of Journalism," 13.

25. Ray Stannard Baker, *American Chronicle: The Autobiography of Ray Stannard Baker*, 47.

26. Charles Edward Russell, *These Shifting Scenes*, 69.

27. Florence Finch Kelly, *Flowing Stream: The Story of Fifty-Six Years in American Newspaper Life*, 197.

28. Elizabeth G. Jordan, *Three Rousing Cheers*, 27.

29. Coates, "Paying City Journalism," 12; "The Real Reporter," 6.

30. William Henry Smith, "The Press as News Gatherer," 526.

31. George Alfred Townsend, "Hearing My Requiem [Journalist Series]," 494.

32. Franklin Matthews, "A Night in a Metropolitan Newspaper Office," 332–36.

33. Shuman, *Steps Into Journalism*, 109.

34. Albert Franklin Matthews, "The Metropolitan Newspaper Reporter," 164–68.

35. Shuman, *Steps Into Journalism*, 101–2.

36. Alex G. Nevins, "The Blue Pencil and How to Avoid It," 12.

37. Robert Luce, *Writing for the Press: A Manual for Editors, Reporters, Correspondents, and Printers*, 4th ed., 54.

38. Randall S. Sumpter, "'Practical Reporting': Late Nineteenth-Century Journalistic Standards and Rule Breaking," 44–64.

39. Ibid.

40. Fedler, *Lessons from the Past*, 83–100.

41. Matthews, "The Metropolitan Newspaper Reporter," 164–68.

42. Janet E. Steele, *The Sun Shines for All: Journalism and Ideology in the Life of Charles A. Dana*; Frank M. O'Brien, *The Story of the Sun*; Candace Stone, *Dana and the Sun*; Will Irwin, *The Making of a Reporter*; Matthews, "The Metropolitan Newspaper Reporter," 164–68.

43. O'Brien, *The Story of the Sun*, 316.

44. Ibid., 321.

45. Steele, *The Sun Shines for All*, 158.

46. Stone, *Dana and the Sun*, 53.

47. O'Brien, *The Story of the Sun*, 268.

48. Julius Chambers, "Chats About Journalism," 5.

49. John W. Perry, "A Newspaper Visit to the 1884 Scene," sec. 2, 292–93.

50. Ibid., 292.

51. Besides *New York Times* obituaries, these reference works were used: Joseph P. McKerns, ed., *Biographical Dictionary of American Journalism*; Perry J. Ashley, ed., *Dictionary of Literary Biography*, vol. 25; *National Cyclopedia of American Biography, 1892–1947*, vols. 11, 18, 32; Peter Hastings Falk, ed., *Who Was Who in American Art, 1564–1975*, 3 vols.; *Who Was Who Among North American Authors, 1921–1939*, 2 vols.; W. J. Burke and Will D. Howe, *American Authors and Books, 1640–1940*; *Who Was Who in America, 1897–1942, vol. 1*; W. Stewart Wallace, *A Dictionary of North American Authors Deceased Before 1960*; M. N. Ask and S. Gershanek, comp., *Who Was Who in Journalism, 1925–1928*, Gale Composite Biographical Dictionary Series, no. 4; John A. Garraty, ed., and Jerome L. Sternstein, associate ed., *Encyclopedia of American Biography*; Robert B. Downs and Jane B. Downs, *Journalists of the United States: Biographical Sketches of Print and Broadcast News Shapers from the Late 17th Century to the Present*; *Who's Who in America.*

52. Samuel G. Blythe, *The Making of a Newspaper Man*, 220.

53. Shuman, *Steps Into Journalism*, 49.

54. Augustus Thomas, *The Print of My Remembrance*, 202.

55. Mencken, *Newspaper Days*, 14.

56. Isaac F. Marcosson, *Adventures in Interviewing*, 17.

57. Kelly, *Flowing Stream*, 140.

58. Frederick Palmer, *With My Own Eyes: A Personal Story of Battle Years*, 18.

59. Moses Koenigsberg, *King News: An Autobiography*, 58.

60. Cobb, *Exit Laughing*, 142.

61. Russell, *These Shifting Scenes*, 274–75.

62. Ibid., 292–93.

63. Ibid.

64. William Allen White, *The Autobiography of William Allen White*, 132; William Salisbury, *The Career of a Journalist*, 8.

65. Jordan, *Three Rousing Cheers*, 28.

66. Kelly, *Flowing Stream*; Henry H. Klein, *My Last 50 Years: An Autobiographical History of "Inside" New York*.

67. Jordan, *Three Rousing Cheers*, 36; Thomas, *The Print of My Remembrance*, 211.

68. Stephen Bonsal, *Heyday in a Vanished World*, 15.

69. Salisbury, *Career of a Journalist*, 8.

70. Thomas, *The Print of My Remembrance*, 198.

71. Russell, *These Shifting Scenes*, 63.

72. Irwin, *The Making of a Reporter*, 50.

73. Marcosson, *Adventures in Interviewing*, 30; Bonsal, *Heyday in a Vanished World*, 411; Beatrice Fairfax [Marie Manning], *Ladies Now and Then*, 9.

74. Ralph D. Paine, *Roads of Adventure*, 129.

75. Ibid., 128.

76. Kelly, *Flowing Stream*, 139.

77. Rheta Childe Dorr, *A Woman of Fifty*, 148.

78. Baker, *American Chronicle*, 81.

79. Mitchell, *Memoirs of an Editor*, 98–125.

80. Paine, *Roads of Adventure*, 32.

81. Koenigsberg, *King News*, 13; White, *Autobiography*, 140.

82. Cobb, *Exit Laughing*, 102.

83. Ibid., 103.

84. Ibid., 104.

85. Baker, *American Chronicle*, 15.

86. Lincoln Steffens, *The Autobiography of Lincoln Steffens, Complete in One Volume*, 202-7.

## Chapter Five. Interviewers and Sources

1. E. L. Shuman, *Steps Into Journalism: Helps and Hints for Young Writers*, 59.

2. "Rights of Interviewers," 4.

3. G. C. Mathews, "The Reporter," 7.

4. Charles Dudley Warner, "Charles Dudley Warner Tells Some Hurting Truths of the Press," 3. In 1873, Warner co-authored *The Gilded Age: A Tale of*

*Today* with Mark Twain. Warner edited the *Hartford Press* and the consolidated *Hartford Press and Courant* before becoming a book author and magazine contributor.

5. Shuman, *Steps Into Journalism*, 68; Frank A. Burr, "The Art of Interviewing," 392; Philip G. Hubert Jr., "An Interviewer on Interviewing," 392–400; Michael Schudson, "Question Authority: A History of the News Interview in American Journalism, 1860s–1930s," 565–87.

6. Schudson, "Question Authority," 565–87; Mitchell Stephens, *A History of News*, 3rd ed., 230–33.

7. Schudson, "Question Authority," 565.

8. Burr, "Art of Interviewing," 395; Hubert, "Interviewer on Interviewing," 392; David S. Barry, "News-Getting at the Capital," 282–86.

9. Hubert, "Interviewer on Interviewing," 392.

10. Ibid., 396–97.

11. Ibid., 393.

12. Betty Houchin Winfield and Janice Hume, "The American Hero and the Evolution of the Human Interest Story," 79–99.

13. Mark Sullivan, *The Education of an American*, 120; Samuel G. Blythe, *The Making of a Newspaper Man*, 36; John Palmer Gavit, "What Is News? Sources of News, Tricks of the Trade, and Hints on Ways and Means," 11.

14. Horace Townsend, "Interviewing as a Factor in Journalism," 522–23.

15. Shuman, *Steps Into Journalism*, 68.

16. Elizabeth L. Banks, *The Autobiography of a "Newspaper Girl,"* 287.

17. Beatrice Fairfax [Marie Manning], *Ladies Now and Then*, 28.

18. Paul Collins, *The Murder of the Century: The Gilded Age Crime that Scandalized a City & Sparked the Tabloid Wars.*

19. Burr, "The Art of Interviewing," 398, 391–402.

20. Barry, "News-Getting at the Capital," 283.

21. Ibid., 282–86.

22. Moses Koenigsberg, *King News: An Autobiography*, 92–93.

23. Fairfax, *Ladies Now and Then*, 16.

24. Charles Edward Russell, *These Shifting Scenes*, 264–65.

25. Augustus Thomas, *The Print of My Remembrance*, 207–24.

26. Moses P. Handy, "A Special Correspondent's Story. The Surrender of the *Virginius*. [Journalist Series]," 757–65.

27. Lincoln Steffens, *The Autobiography of Lincoln Steffens: Complete in One Volume*, 186.

28. Elizabeth G. Jordan, *Three Rousing Cheers*, 33; Banks, *The Autobiography of a "Newspaper Girl,"* 202.

29. Banks, *The Autobiography of a "Newspaper Girl,"* 201.

30. Florence Finch Kelly, *Flowing Stream: The Story of Fifty-Six Years in American Newspaper Life*, 172.

31. Steffens, *The Autobiography of Lincoln Steffens*, 183.

32. Ibid., 184.

33. Ibid., 182.

34. Alexander Dana Noyes, *The Market Place: Reminiscences of a Financial Editor*, 51.

35. Isaac Marcosson, *Adventures in Interviewing*, 50.

36. Ibid.

37. Ibid., 74–76.

38. Ibid., 76.

39. Russell, *These Shifting Scenes*, 294.

40. Banks, *Autobiography of a "Newspaper Girl,"* 288.

41. Ibid., 289.

42. Russell, *These Shifting Scenes*, 40.

43. Shuman, *Steps Into Journalism*, 70.

44. Ibid., 71.

45. Nellie Bly, "Nellie Bly Again. She Interviews Emma Goldman. And Other Anarchists," 1.

46. Ibid., 3.

47. Ibid.

48. Ibid.

49. "Two Girl Heroines Save Children's Lives," 7.

50. Shuman, *Steps Into Journalism*, 180.

51. Hubert, "Interviewer on Interviewing," 394.

52. A. E. Watrous, "The Newspaper-Man as a Confidant. [Journalist Series.]," 332–35; Shuman, *Steps Into Journalism*, 104.

53. John Palmer Gavit, "What Is News? A Manual for Newspaper Reporters and Correspondents," 12.

54. Cynthia E. Cleveland, "Women in Washington as Newspaper Correspondents," 602.

55. Lincoln Steffens, *The Autobiography of Lincoln Steffens*, 186.

56. J. B. McCormick, "The Sporting Editor. [Journalist Series]," 638.

57. Ibid.

## Chapter Six. Career Models in Newspaper Fiction

1. These results were compiled from several searches of the USC Annenberg's Image of the Journalist in Popular Culture databases. See http://www.ijpc.org.

2. James L. Ford, *Forty-Odd Years in the Literary Shop*, 123.

3. Howard Good, *Acquainted with the Night: The Image of Journalists in American Fiction, 1890–1930*; Karen Roggenkamp, "Elizabeth Jordan, 'True

Stories of the News,' and Newspaper Fiction in Late Nineteenth-Century Journalism," in *Literature and Journalism: Inspirations, Intersections, and Inventions from Ben Franklin to Stephen Colbert*, ed. Mark Canada, 119–41.

4. "Scoresby's Mistake: A 'Newspaper' Story," 286–90.

5. Good, *Acquainted with the Night*, 87.

6. "Scoresby's Mistake," 286.

7. The stories in these three volumes were first published as stand-alone short stories, making it difficult to calculate how many versions of these texts were sold. Charles Scribner's Sons printed 40,000 copies of *Gallegher and Other Stories* in book form between 1891 and 1897. See "Among the Books," 865.

8. H. L. Mencken, *Newspaper Days: 1899–1906*, 12.

9. "Recent Fiction," 20.

10. "Tales of the City Room," 266.

11. "Chronicle and Comment," 291–310.

12. "Book-Talk: Books Received," 436–40.

13. "Bookishness: Cosmopolitan Literary Juggling," 299.

14. "Richard Harding Davis," 422–23; "Elizabeth Garver Jordan," 270–71; "Jesse Lynch Williams," 469–70.

15. John Kaler, "James Otis Kaler: A Biographical Sketch," 183–211; Ray Stannard Baker, *American Chronicle: The Autobiography of Ray Stannard Baker*; "Kirk Munroe, Author, Dies in Miami at 69," 24.

16. Will Irwin, *The Making of a Reporter*, 109.

17. Ibid., 31.

18. Jesse Lynch Williams, *The Stolen Story and Other Newspaper Stories*, 69.

19. Ibid., 219–20.

20. Ibid., 87.

21. Ray Stannard Baker, "Pippins," 435.

22. Williams, *The Stolen Story*, 253; Kirk Munroe, *Under Orders: The Story of a Young Reporter*; Elizabeth Garver Jordan, *Tales of the City Room*. Stories about Billings, Woods, and Herrick appear in most, if not all, story collections about journalists.

23. Williams, *The Stolen Story*, 129.

24. Munroe, *Under Orders*, 34.

25. Williams, *The Stolen Story*, 22.

26. Ibid., 245.

27. Ibid., 4.

28. Jordan, *Tales of the City Room*, 17–29.

29. Williams, *The Stolen Story*, 120.

30. Ibid., 247.

31. Ibid., 235.

32. Ibid., 67–68.

33. Baker, "Pippins," 435.

34. Williams, *The Stolen Story*, 127–59.

35. Munroe, *Under Orders*, 347.

36. Jordan, *Tales of the City Room*, 109.

37. Ibid., 196.

38. Haryot Holt Cahoon, "Women in Gutter Journalism," 568.

39. Jordan, *Tales of the City Room*, 213.

40. Ibid., 227.

41. James L. Ford, "The Story of the Young Man of Talent," 10.

42. James L. Ford, "Hypnotic Tales," 148.

43. James L. Ford, "Our Village: III. Our Literary Circles," 120–21.

44. James L. Ford, "The Great Yellow Way: With Abject Apologies to James Creelman," 348.

45. Richard Harding Davis, *Gallegher and Other Stories*, 5.

46. James Otis Kaler, *Jenny Wren's Boarding-House: A Story of Newsboy Life in New York*, 70.

47. Ibid., 132.

48. Adams would use those themes in four novels. See Samuel Hopkins Adams, *The Clarion*; Samuel Hopkins Adams, *Average Jones*; Samuel Hopkins Adams, *Common Cause: A Novel of the War in America*; Samuel Hopkins Adams, *Success: A Novel.*

49. Adams, *The Clarion*, 47.

50. Ibid., 94.

51. Ibid., 99.

52. Ibid., 100.

53. Ibid., 221.

54. Will Irwin, *Warrior the Untamed: The Story of an Imaginative Press Agent*, 231.

55. Ibid., 32–33.

56. J. B. Montgomery-M'Govern, "An Important Phase of Gutter Journalism: Faking," 240.

57. Williams, *The Stolen Story*, 187.

58. Ibid., 214.

59. "Sensational Journalism," 12; Christopher P. Wilson, *The Labor of Words: Literary Professionalism in the Progressive Era*, 35.

## Chapter Seven. The Rule Breakers

1. Ted Curtis Smythe, *The Gilded Age Press, 1865–1900*, 155; Fred Fedler, *Lessons from the Past: Journalists' Lives and Work, 1850–1950*, 111–13; Gerald J. Baldasty, *The Commercialization of News in the Nineteenth Century*, 90;

Randall S. Sumpter, "'Practical Reporting': Late Nineteenth-Century Journalistic Standards and Rule Breaking," 44–64.

2. Elizabeth Garver Jordan, *Tales of the City Room*, unpaged notes.

3. Andie Tucher, "The True, The False, and The 'Not Exactly Lying,'" in *Literature and Journalism: Inspirations, Intersections and Inventions from Ben Franklin to Stephen Colbert*, ed. Mark Canada, 92.

4. George Grantham Bain, "Newspaper 'Faking,'" 274.

5. J. B. Montgomery-M'Govern, "An Important Phase of Gutter Journalism: Faking," 240.

6. "General Metropolitan News, Startled by a Newspaper 'Fake,'" 11.

7. "A Lion 'Escapes' in a Stable," 8.

8. E. W. B., "Chapter on the Bustle: It Was Discarded as the Result of a Newspaper Romance," 4.

9. "Items of General News," 3.

10. Justin T. Clark, "Confronting the 'Seeker of Newspaper Notoriety': Pathological Lying, the Public, and the Press, 1890–1920," 179–200; Sterling Heilig, "King of Art Fakers Is Coming Here to Expose Fake Paintings in American Galleries," 4.

11. Aviva Briefel, *The Deceivers: Art Forgery and Identity in the Nineteenth Century*, 5.

12. Abigail Baker, "The Ithaca Jewel: An Authentic Fake," 97–108.

13. "Factories of 'Antiquities,'" 3; R. S., "Trade in Spurious Art," 4.

14. E. L. Shuman, *Steps Into Journalism: Helps and Hints for Young Writers*, 122. Shuman modified his viewpoint in a later publication that dealt more harshly with faking.

15. Bain, "Newspaper 'Faking,'" 274–79.

16. William Salisbury, The *Career of a Journalist*, 58.

17. Mark Sullivan, *The Education of an American*, 122–23.

18. Sullivan, *Education of an American*, 126.

19. Julian Ralph, *The Making of a Journalist*, 23.

20. Florence Finch Kelly, *Flowing Stream: The Story of Fifty-Six Years in American Newspaper Life*, 170.

21. Shuman, *Steps Into Journalism*, 123.

22. Samuel G. Blythe, *The Making of a Newspaper Man*, 175.

23. Kelly, *Flowing Stream*, 199.

24. "Sensational Journalism," 12.

25. Montgomery-M'Govern, "Important Phase," 240–54.

26. Blythe, *The Making of a Newspaper Man*, 42–43.

27. Isaac F. Marcosson, *Adventures in Interviewing*, 23–24; William Salisbury, *The Career of a Journalist*, 38; Kent Cooper, *Kent Cooper and the Associated Press: An Autobiography*, 13–15.

28. Montgomery-M'Govern, "Important Phase," 255.
29. Fedler, *Lessons from the Past*, 111–13.
30. Seyon [pseud.], "News-Gathering in Washington," 452–54.
31. Ibid., 452.
32. Edward P. Mitchell, *Memoirs of an Editor: Fifty Years of American Journalism*, 80.
33. Will Irwin, *The Making of a Reporter*, 52.
34. Augustus Thomas, *Print of My Remembrance*, 193.
35. Salisbury, *Career of a Journalist*, 6.
36. Lincoln Steffens, *Autobiography of Lincoln Steffens: Complete in One Volume*, 204.
37. Moses Koenigsberg, *King News: An Autobiography*, 95–96.
38. Elizabeth L. Banks, *The Autobiography of a "Newspaper Girl"*, 207.
39. Ibid., 44–45.
40. Ibid., 49.
41. Ibid., 209, 72.
42. Alexander Dana Noyes, *The Market Place: Reminiscences of a Financial Editor*, 67.
43. Banks, *Autobiography of a "Newspaper Girl,"* 206.
44. Ibid., 207.
45. Ralph, *Making of a Journalist*, 37.
46. Harry Thurston Peck, "A Great National Newspaper," 220.
47. "The Influence of the Newspapers," 3.
48. "Hints to Journalists," March 22, 1884, 2.
49. "Hints to Journalists," June 13, 1885, 6.
50. Matthew Unit, "Room at the Top?" 1.
51. John Brisben Walker, "Some Difficulties of Modern Journalism," 328.
52. "The Rights of the Blue Pencil," 8.
53. "Severe Discipline," 6.
54. Ray Stannard Baker, *American Chronicle: The Autobiography of Ray Stannard Baker*, 22.
55. Matthew Unit, "Explanatory Journalism," 1.
56. Moses Koenigsberg, *King News: An Autobiography*, 502.

## Chapter Eight. Conclusion

1. Irvin S. Cobb, *Exit Laughing*, 142.
2. Randall S. Sumpter, "Core Knowledge: Early Reporting Textbooks and the Formation of Professional Identity," 42–51.
3. The books are: Willard Grosvenor Bleyer, *Newspaper Writing and Editing*; H. F. Harrington and T. T. Frankenberg, *Essentials in Journalism: A Manual in*

*Newspaper Making for College Classes*; Grant Milnor Hyde, *Newspaper Reporting and Correspondence: A Manual for Reporters, Correspondents, and Students of Newspaper Writing*; Charles G. Ross, *The Writing of News: A Handbook with Chapters on Newspaper Correspondence and Copy Reading*; M. Lyle Spencer, *News Writing: The Gathering, Handling and Writing of News Stories.*

4. Sumpter, "Core Knowledge," 42–51.

5. Florence Finch Kelly, *Flowing Stream: The Story of Fifty-Six Years in American Newspaper Life*, 201.

6. James Salazar, *Bodies of Reform: The Rhetoric of Character in Gilded Age America,* 9.

7. "The Serious Side of the American Character," 326.

8. David Traxel, *Crusader Nation: The United States in Peace and the Great War, 1898–1920,* 6.

9. Paul S. Boyer, *Purity in Print: Book Censorship in America from the Gilded Age to the Computer Age*, 3, 5.

10. Albert Bushnell Hart, "American Character in Politics," 142–46.

11. Lincoln Steffens, *The Autobiography of Lincoln Steffens: Complete in One Volume*, 180.

12. Warren Breed, "Social Control in the Newsroom: A Functional Analysis," 326–35.

13. Herbert J. Gans, *Deciding What's News: A Study of CBS Evening News, NBC Nightly News, Newsweek and Time*, 42–55.

14. Brian McNair, *The Sociology of Journalism*, 6.

15. Michael Schudson, *The Sociology of News*, 2nd ed; R. M. Entman, "Framing: Toward Clarification of a Fractured Paradigm," 51–58.

16. Mark Fishman, *Manufacturing the News*, 21–23.

17. Edward P. Mitchell, *Memoirs of an Editor: Fifty Years of American Journalism*, 80.

18. Gaye Tuchman, *Making News: A Study in the Construction of Reality*, 23.

19. Fishman, *Manufacturing the News*, 23.

20. Will Irwin, *The Making of a Reporter*, 52.

21. Fishman, *Manufacturing the News*, 23–24.

22. Phyllis C. Kaniss, *Making Local News*, 222.

23. Fishman, *Manufacturing the News*, 92.

24. Tuchman, *Making News,* 106.

25. Irvin S. Cobb, *Exit Laughing*, 142.

26. Craig Silverman, "A New Age for Truth," 4–7.

27. Borja Echevarría de la Gándara, "New Challenges, New Rewards," 31–32.

28. Paul Farhi, "Mistaken Nation," 32–37.

29. Mathew Ingram, "What a Map of the Fake-News Ecosystem Says about the Problem," *Fortune.com*, last modified November 28, 2016, http://fortune.com/2016/11/28/map-fake-news/.

30. Lars Willnat and David H. Weaver, "The American Journalist in the Digital Age: Key Findings" (paper presented at the annual meeting of the Association for Education in Journalism and Mass Communication, Chicago, Ill., August 2017), 1–27. Weaver and co-investigators have conducted similar surveys in 1982, 1992, 2002, and 2013.

31. Stephen Quinn, *Convergent Journalism: The Fundamentals of Multimedia Reporting*, 153–76.

32. Willnat and Weaver, "The American Journalist," 3.

33. Ibid., 13.

34. Ibid.

35. Ebsco's Communication and Mass Media Complete database yielded those results.

36. Amy Schmitz Weiss and David Domingo, "Innovation Processes in Online Newsrooms as Actor-Networks and Communities of Practice," 1156–71; José Alberto García-Avilés, "Online Newsrooms as Communities of Practice: Exploring Digital Journalists' Applied Ethics," 258–72.

37. Quinn, *Convergent Journalism*, 153–76.

38. Doug Tewksbury, "Online-Offline Knowledge Sharing in the Occupy Movement: Howtooccupy.org and Discursive Communities of Practice," 11–23.

# Bibliography


### Primary Sources, Books

Adams, Samuel Hopkins. *Average Jones*. Indianapolis: Bobbs-Merrill Co., 1911.

———. *The Clarion*. Boston & New York: Houghton Mifflin Co., 1914.

———. *Common Cause: A Novel of the War in America*. Boston & New York: Houghton Mifflin Co., 1919.

———. *Success: A Novel*. Boston & New York: Houghton Mifflin Co., 1921.

An Editor, by [pseud.]. Preface to *Hints to Young Editors*. New Haven, Conn.: Charles C. Chatfield & Co., 1872.

Baker, Ray Stannard. *American Chronicle: The Autobiography of Ray Stannard Baker*. New York: Charles Scribner's Sons, 1945.

Banks, Elizabeth L. *The Autobiography of a "Newspaper Girl."* London: Methuen & Co., 1902.

Bleyer, Willard Grosvenor. *Newspaper Writing and Editing*. Boston: Houghton Mifflin Co., 1913.

Blythe, Samuel G. *The Making of a Newspaper Man*. 1912. Reprint, Westport, Conn.: Greenwood Press, 1970.

Bonsal, Stephen. *Heyday in a Vanished World*. New York: W. W. Norton & Co. Inc., 1937.

Cobb, Irvin S. *Exit Laughing*. 1941. Reprint, Detroit: Gale Research Co., 1974.

Cooper, Kent. *Kent Cooper and the Associated Press: An Autobiography*. New York: Random House, 1959.

Crawshaw, W. H. *The Interpretation of Literature*. New York: Macmillan & Co., 1896.

Cropper, Frank. *The Amateur Journalists' Companion*. Louisville, Ky.: Frank Cropper, Publisher, 1873.

Davis, Richard Harding. *Gallegher and Other Stories*. 1891. Reprint, New York: Garrett Press Inc., 1968.

Dorr, Rheta Childe. *A Woman of Fifty*. New York & London: Funk & Wagnalls Co., 1924.

Dreiser, Theodore. *A History of Myself: Newspaper Days*. 7th ed. New York: Horace Liveright, Inc., 1931.

Fairfax, Beatrice [Marie Manning]. *Ladies Now and Then*. New York: E. P. Dutton & Co., Inc., 1944.

Ford, James L. *Forty-Odd Years in the Literary Shop*. New York: E. P. Dutton Co., 1921.

Gaskell, G. A. *How to Write for the Press*. New York: Office of the "Penman Gazette," 1884.

Harrington, H. F., and T. T. Frankenberg. *Essentials in Journalism: A Manual in Newspaper Making for College Classes*. Boston: Ginn & Co., 1912.

Hill, Adams Sherman. *Our English*. New York: Harper & Brothers, 1888.

Hyde, Grant Milnor. *Newspaper Reporting and Correspondence: A Manual for Reporters, Correspondents, and Students of Newspaper Writing*. New York: D. Appleton & Co., 1912.

Irwin, Will. *Warrior the Untamed: The Story of an Imaginative Press Agent*. New York: Doubleday, Page & Co., 1909.

———. *The Making of a Reporter*. New York: G. P. Putnam's Sons, 1942.

Jordan, Elizabeth Garver. *Tales of the City Room*. 1898. Reprint, Freeport, N.Y.: Books for Libraries Press, 1970.

———. *Three Rousing Cheers*. New York & London: D. Appleton-Century Co., 1938.

Kelly, Florence Finch. *Flowing Stream: The Story of Fifty-Six Years in American Newspaper Life*. New York: E. P. Dutton, 1939.

Klein, Henry H. *My Last 50 Years: An Autobiographical History of "Inside" New York*. New York: Isaac Goldman Co., 1935.

Koenigsberg, Moses. *King News: An Autobiography*. 1941. Reprint, New York: Books for Libraries, 1972.

Luby, James. *James Luby, Journalist*. Washington, D.C.: Ransdell Inc., 1930.

Luce, Robert. *Writing for the Press: A Manual for Editors, Reporters, Correspondents, and Printers*. 4th ed. Revised and enlarged. Boston: The Writer Publishing Co., 1891.

Marcosson, Isaac F. *Adventures in Interviewing*. New York: John Lane Co., 1919.

Mencken, H. L. *Newspaper Days, 1899–1906*. New York: Alfred A. Knopf, 1941.

Mitchell, Edward P. *Memoirs of an Editor: Fifty Years of American Journalism*. New York: Charles Scribner's Sons, 1924.

Munroe, Kirk. *Under Orders: The Story of a Young Reporter*. New York: G. P. Putnam's Sons, 1890.

Nixon, John Travis, comp. *A History of the National Amateur Press Association*. Crowley, La.: The Mirror Print, 1900.

Noyes, Alexander Dana. *The Market Place: Reminiscences of a Financial Editor.* Boston: Little, Brown & Co., 1938.

*N. W. Ayer & Son's American Newspaper Annual.* Philadelphia: N. W. Ayer & Son, 1888.

*N. W. Ayer & Son's American Newspaper Annual.* Philadelphia: N. W. Ayer & Son, 1890.

*N. W. Ayer & Son's American Newspaper Annual.* Philadelphia: N. W. Ayer & Son, 1894.

O'Brien, Frank M. *The Story of the Sun.* New York: George H. Doran Co., 1918.

Older, Fremont. *My Own Story.* New York: Macmillan, 1926.

Otis, James. *Jenny Wren's Boarding-House: A Story of Newsboy Life in New York.* Boston: Dana Estes & Co., 1893.

Paine, Ralph Delahaye. *Roads of Adventure.* Boston & New York: Houghton Mifflin Co., 1922.

Palmer, Frederick. *With My Own Eyes: A Personal Story of Battle Years.* Indianapolis, Ind.: Bobbs-Merrill Co., 1933.

Ralph, Julian. *The Making of a Journalist.* New York & London: Harper & Brothers Publishers, 1903.

Rayne, Martha L. *What Can a Woman Do: Her Position in the Business and Literary World.* 1893. Reprint, New York: Arno Press Inc., 1974.

Rogers, James Edwards. *The American Newspaper.* Chicago: University of Chicago, 1910.

Ross, Charles G. *The Writing of News: A Handbook with Chapters on Newspaper Correspondence and Copy Reading.* New York: Henry Holt & Co., 1911.

Russell, Charles Edward. *These Shifting Scenes.* New York: George H. Doran Co., 1914.

Salisbury, William. *The Career of a Journalist.* New York: B. W. Dodge, 1908.

Shuman, E. L. *Steps Into Journalism: Helps and Hints for Young Writers.* Evanston, Ill.: Evanston Press Co., Printers, 1894.

Spencer, M. Lyle. *News Writing: The Gathering, Handling and Writing of News Stories.* Boston: D. C. Heath & Co., 1917.

Steffens, Lincoln. *The Autobiography of Lincoln Steffens: Complete in One Volume.* New York: Harcourt, Brace, 1931.

Sullivan, Mark. *The Education of an American.* New York: Doubleday, Doran & Co. Inc., 1938.

Thomas, Augustus. *The Print of My Remembrance.* New York: Charles Scribner's Sons, 1922.

Trent, William P. *The Authority of Criticism and Other Essays.* New York: Charles Scribner's Sons, 1899.

Vincent, John H. *The Chautauqua Movement.* 1886. Reprint, Freeport, N.Y.: Books for Libraries Press, 1971.

White, William Allen. *The Autobiography of William Allen White.* New York: Macmillan, 1946.

Williams, Jesse Lynch. *The Stolen Story and Other Newspaper Stories.* 1899. Reprint, Freeport, N.Y.: Books for Libraries Press, 1969.

## Primary Sources, Articles

A.F. "The Linotype and the Man Who Made It." *The Journalist,* August 8, 1891, 2–3.

"Among the Books." *New York Observer and Chronicle,* December 23, 1897, 865.

An Every Day Scribbler [pseud.]. "The Scribbler and His Paymaster." *The Independent,* August 8, 1901, 1840–44.

Arden, Edward. "The Evolution of the Newspaper." *Chautauquan,* May 1899, 152–54.

Armstrong, F. Leroy. "The Daily Papers of Chicago." *Chautauquan,* August 1898, 538–45.

Avenel, Walter. "Journalism as a Profession." *Forum,* May 1898, 366–74.

Bain, George Grantham. "Newspaper 'Faking.'" *Lippincott's Monthly Magazine,* August 1894, 274–78.

Baker, Ray Stannard. "Pippins." *The Youth's Companion,* September 7, 1899, 435.

Barry, David S. "News-Getting at the Capital." *Chautauquan,* December 1897, 282–86.

Barry, John D. "New York Letter." *The Literary World; A Monthly Review of Current Literature,* April 16, 1898, 120–21.

Blowitz, Henri de. "The Profession: There Are Others, But They Are Not 'In It.'" *Fourth Estate,* November 7, 1895, 8.

Bly, Nellie. "Nellie Bly Again. She Interviews Emma Goldman and Other Anarchists." *New York World,* September 17, 1893, 1, 3.

"Book Table: The Newest Books." *New York Evangelist,* November 5, 1896, 11.

"Book-Talk: Books Received." *The Nassau Literary Magazine,* March 1898, 436–40.

"Bookishness: Cosmopolitan Literary Juggling." *Life,* April 7, 1898, 298.

Brisbane, Arthur. "How to Be a Better Newspaperman: Famous Editor Gives the Ten Most Important Newspaper Rules." New York: King Features Syndicate Inc., 1930.

Burr, Frank A. "The Art of Interviewing." *Lippincott's Monthly Magazine,* September 1890, 391–402.

Cahoon, Haryot Holt. "Women in Gutter Journalism." *Arena*, March 1897, 568–76.

Campbell-Copeland, T. "Ladder of Journalism: How to Climb It." *The Journalist*, May 11, 1889, 13.

———. "Ladder of Journalism: How to Climb It." *The Journalist*, July 13, 1889, 13.

"Chairs of Journalism." *The Journalist*, October 16, 1886, 4.

Chambers, Julius. "The Managing Editor. [Journalist Series]." *Lippincott's Monthly Magazine*. February 1892, 195–202.

———. "Chats about Journalism." *Once A Week: An Illustrated Weekly Newspaper*, May 31, 1892, 5.

"Christmas Journal Chief Triumph of Printing Art." *New York Journal & Advertiser*, December 10, 1899, 58.

"Chronicle and Comment." *The Bookman; a Review of Books and Life*, June 1899, 291–310.

Clark, S. N. "The Associated Press." *Chautauquan*, November 1886, 79–82.

Cleveland, Cynthia E. "Women in Washington as Newspaper Correspondents." *Chautauquan*, February 1894, 601–2.

Coates, Foster. "Paying City Journalism." *The Journalist*, December 24, 1887, 12.

Cockerill, John A. "The Newspaper of the Future: [Journalist Series]." *Lippincott's Monthly Magazine*, August 1892, 220–26.

"College of Journalism." *The Journalist*, March 20, 1886, 4.

"Country Newspaper, The." *Fourth Estate*, January 10, 1895, 5.

"Current Topics." *The Youth's Companion*, March 4, 1897, 102.

Curtis, David A. "Tips for the Boys." *The Journalist*, August 18, 1894, 7.

D. [pseudo.]. "A Man Who Has a Theory." *New York Times*, September 20, 1898, 6.

"Deadly Parallel, The." *Los Angeles Times*, June 19, 1892, 5.

Duffield, Pitts. "A Modest Proposal Touching the Newspapers And An American Academy." *The Chap-Book*, November 1, 1897, 447.

E. W. B. "A Chapter on the Bustle: It Was Discarded as the Results of a Newspaper Romance." *Atlanta Constitution*, November 7, 1892, 4.

Editor of the Journalist [pseud.]. "One of Many." *The Journalist*, December 10, 1887, 6.

"Editor's Assistant, The." *Fourth Estate*, March 29, 1894, 6.

"Editorial Comment." *Atlanta Constitution*, January 20, 1894, 4.

"Editorial Policy of Trade Press." *Chicago Daily Tribune*, September 21, 1896, 3.

"Employments for Boys." *Scientific American*, December 9, 1871, 369.

"Factories of 'Antiquities.'" *New York Times*, March 31, 1903, 3.

Fenton, Frances. "The Influence of Newspaper Presentations Upon the Growth of Crime and Other Anti-Social Activity." *American Journal of Sociology* 16 (November 1910): 342–71.

———. "The Influence of Newspaper Presentations Upon the Growth of Crime and Other Anti-Social Activity." *American Journal of Sociology* 16 (January 1911): 538–64.

Flood, Ned Arden. "The Beginnings of Newspaper Enterprise." *Chautauquan*, July 1899, 331–33.

Ford, James L. "Hypnotic Tales." *Puck*, April 29, 1891, 148.

———. "The Story of the Young Man of Talent." *Puck*, September 13, 1893, 10.

———. "Our Village: III. Our Literary Circles." *Life*, February 21, 1895, 120–21.

———. "The Great Yellow Way: With Abject Apologies to James Creelman." *Life*, October 23, 1902, 348–49.

Forman, Allan. Introduction to "The Blue Pencil and How to Avoid It," by Alex G. Nevins. *The Journalist*, April 26, 1890, 12.

"'Forum' for August, The." *New York Times*, July 28, 1893, 4.

French, E. M. C. "Study Your Paper." *The Journalist*, December 14, 1889, 30.

"Future of Newspapers, The." *Newspaperdom*, June–July 1893, 152.

Gavit, John Palmer. "What Is News? A Manual for Newspaper Reporters and Correspondents." *The Journalist*, April 23, 1892, 12–13.

———."What Is News? A Manual for Newspaper Reporters and Correspondents." *The Journalist*, April 30, 1892, 14.

———. "What Is News? Sources of News, 'Tricks of The Trade', And Hints on Ways and Means." *The Journalist*, August 13, 1892, 10–11.

"General Metropolitan News, Startled by a Newspaper 'Fake.'" *Chicago Daily Tribune*, December 30, 1888, 11.

"Get News of Trade." *Chicago Daily Tribune*, February 24, 1894, 4.

Gilder, Jeannette L. "Journalism for Girls." *The Youth's Companion*, December 17, 1891, 656A.

Halstead, Murat. "Early Editorial Experiences: [Journalist Series]." *Lippincott's Monthly Magazine*, June 1892, 710–15.

Handy, Moses P. "A Special Correspondent's Story. The Surrender of the *Virginius*. [Journalist Series]." *Lippincott's Monthly Magazine*, December 1892, 757–65.

Hapgood, Norman. "American Art Criticism." *The Bookman; A Review of Books and Life*, September 1897, 45–47.

Hart, Albert Bushnell. "American Character in Politics." *Chautauquan*, November 1895, 142–46.

Heilig, Sterling. "King of Art Fakers is Coming Here to Expose Fake Paintings in American Galleries." *The New York Sun*, April 5, 1903, 4.

"Hints to Journalists." *The Journalist*, March 22, 1884, 2.
"Hints to Journalists." *The Journalist*, June 13, 1885, 6.
Howells, W. D. "Authors and Authorship: The Man of Letters as a Man of Business." *Scribner's Magazine*, October 1893, 429–46.
Hubert, Philip G., Jr. "An Interviewer on Interviewing." *Forum*, December 1886, 392–400.
"In and Around New York." *Congregationalist*, July 27, 1899, 115.
"Influence of Editors." *Fourth Estate*, April 26, 1894, 3–4.
"Influence of The Newspapers, The." *Fourth Estate*, August 23, 1894, 3.
"Interviewer Interviewed: A Talk with 'Gath', An." *Lippincott's Monthly Magazine*, November 1891, 630–38.
"Items of General News." *Maine Farmer*, October 15, 1891, 3.
Jordan, Elizabeth G. "The Newspaper Woman's Story." [Journalist Series]." *Lippincott's Monthly Magazine*, March 1893, 340–47.
———. "What It Means to Be a Newspaper Woman." *The Ladies' Home Journal*, January 1899, 8.
"Journalism and Literature." *Fourth Estate*, May 24, 1894, 4.
"Journalism as a Profession." *The Journalist*, August 1893, 12–13.
Keller, J. W. "Journalism as a Career." *Forum*, August 1893, 691–704.
King, Henry. "The American Press." *Chautauquan*, February 1896, 525–29.
"Lessons in Crime Fifty Cents Per Month." *Outlook*, February 1907, 276–77.
"Linotype." *Fourth Estate*, October 4, 1894, 8.
"Lion 'Escapes' in a Stable, A." *New York Times*, October 27, 1893, 8.
"Making a Journalist." *Fourth Estate*, May 24, 1894, 1, 6.
"Making of a Newspaper, The." *Fourth Estate*. February 28, 1895, 11.
"Mammoth Newspapers, About." *Newspaperdom*, June–July 1893, 152.
Mathews, Byron C. "A Study of a New York Daily." *The Independent*, January 13, 1910, 82–86.
Mathews, G. C. "The Reporter." *The Journalist*, February 28, 1885, 7.
Matthews, Albert Franklin. "Can Practical Newspaper Work Be Taught in College?" *Chautauquan*, April 1893, 48–51.
———. "The Metropolitan Newspaper Reporter." *Chautauquan*, November 1893, 164–68.
Matthews, Franklin. "The Newspaper Press of the United States." *Chautauquan*, November 1894, 162–66.
———. "Newspaper English." *Chautauquan*, June 1895, 302–5.
———. "A Night in a Metropolitan Newspaper Office." *Chautauquan*, June 1896, 332–36.
McClure, A. K. "The Editor-In-Chief: [Journalist Series]." *Lippincott's Monthly Magazine*, January 1892, 77–83.
McCormick, J. B. "The Sporting Editor. [Journalist Series]." *Lippincott's Monthly Magazine*, November 1892, 633–41.

Megargee, Louis N. "A Newspaper Sensation. [Journalist Series]." *Lippincott's Monthly Magazine*. December 1893, 729–36.

Meighan, W. J. C. "The Travelling Correspondent. [Journalist Series]." *Lippincott's Monthly Magazine*, May 1892, 573–80.

Miller, C. R. "A Word to the Critics of Newspapers." *Forum*, August 1893, 712–17.

Montgomery-M'Govern, J. B. "An Important Phase of Gutter Journalism: Faking." *Arena*, February 1898, 240–54.

Nevins, Alex G. "The Blue Pencil and How to Avoid It." *The Journalist*, April 26, 1890, 12–13.

———. "The Blue Pencil and How to Avoid It." *The Journalist*, May 3, 1890, 12–13.

"Newspaper English." *Austin Daily Statesman*, September 30, 1894, 14.

"Newspaper English." *The New York Times*. August 25, 1889, 11.

"Newspaper Ethics." *Current Literature*, June 1898, 483–84.

"Newspaper Symposium, A." *Dial*, August 16, 1893, 79–81.

"Newspaper Women." *Atlanta Constitution*, November 7, 1895, 11.

North, S. N. D. "History and Present Condition of the Newspaper and Periodical Press of the United States." *10th Census of the United States*. Washington: Government Printing Office, 1884.

Norton, T. J. "News, and How to Get It." *Newspaperdom*, October–November 1893, 279.

"Notes." *The Critic: A Weekly Review of Literature and the Arts*, January 26, 1889, 47.

One of the Brotherhood [pseud.]. "The Literary Aspirant." *The Independent*, April 26, 1900, 997–1000.

Palmer, Archie Emerson. "Some Experiences in a Newspaper Office." *Chautauquan*, October 1887, 29–30.

Park, Robert E. "The Natural History of the Newspaper." *American Journal of Sociology* 29, no. 3 (November 1923): 276–89.

———. "The Yellow Press." *Sociology and Social Research* 12, no. 1 (September–October 1927): 3–11.

———. "Reflections on Communication and Culture." *American Journal of Sociology* 44, no. 2 (September 1938): 187–205.

Parton, James. "Journalism as a Profession for Young Men." *Writer*, May 1888, 106–10.

Peck, Harry Thurston. "A Great National Newspaper." *Cosmopolitan; a Monthly Illustrated Magazine*, December 1897, 209–20.

Philips, Melville. "The Literary Editor: [Journalist Series]." *Lippincott's Monthly Magazine*, April 1892, 457–62.

"Playing with the Pen." *Washington Post*, March 9, 1896, 4.

"Primer of Journalism, A." *The Journalist*, August 24, 1889, 8.
Prince, H. "Our Young Contributors: How Harry Got His Printing-Press." *Our Young Folks*, June 1873, 368–71.
"Professorship of Journalism, A." *The Journalist*, July 23, 1887, 2.
R.S. [pseud.]. "Trade in Spurious Art." *New York Times*, April 5, 1903, 4.
"Real Reporter, The." *Fourth Estate*, September 5, 1895, 6.
"Recent Fiction." *Independent*, March 26, 1891, 20.
"Record Broken, A." *Fourth Estate*, March 22, 1894, 1.
"Rights of Interviewers." *Fourth Estate*, October 18, 1894, 4.
"Rights of the Blue Pencil, The." *The Journalist*, April 27, 1889, 8.
Rossiter, William S. "Special Reports on Selected Industries, Printing and Publishing." *12th Census of the United States—Manufactures, Part III.* Washington, D.C.: Government Printing Office, 1902. Reprinted June 1, 1903, 1039–1105.
Sangster, Margaret E. "Editorship as a Profession for Women." *Forum*, December 1895, 445–55.
"Schools of Journalism." *The Journalist*, April 23, 1887, 8.
Schuman, J. G. "Teaching—A Trade or a Profession?" *Forum*, April 1896, 171–85.
"Scoresby's Mistake. A 'Newspaper Story.'" *Frank Leslie's Popular Monthly*, March 1885, 286–90.
"Sensational Journalism." *The Journalist*, August 20, 1892, 12.
"Serious Side of the American Character, The." *Scientific American*, October 31, 1896, 326.
"Severe Discipline." *Fourth Estate*, April 25, 1895, 6.
Seyon [pseud.]. "News-Gathering in Washington. The Special Correspondent." *Chautauquan*, May 1886, 452–54.
Smith, William Henry. "The Press as a News Gatherer." *Century Magazine*, August 1891, 524–26.
"Some Newspaper English." *Outlook*, November 11, 1893, 866.
Speed, John Gilmer. "Do Newspapers Now Give the News?" *Forum*, August 1893, 705–11.
Stanton, Theodore. "The Foreign Correspondent: [Journalist Series]." *Lippincott's Monthly Magazine*, June 1893, 746–52.
"Startled by a Newspaper 'Fake.'" *Chicago Daily Tribune*, December 30, 1888, 11.
Steffens, J. Lincoln. "VI. The Business of a Newspaper. (The Conduct of Great Businesses)." *Scribner's Magazine*, October 1897, 447–67.
"Stories of the Town." *Atlanta Constitution*, February 25, 1896, 4.
Street, Arthur I. "The Truth about the Newspaper." *Chicago Daily Tribune*, July 25, 1909, sec. G, 2.

"Style Book for Proof Readers." *Fourth Estate*, May 26, 1898, 7.

"Tales of the City Room." *The Critic: A Weekly Review of Literature and the Arts*, April 16, 1898, 265–66.

Tenney, Alvan A. "The Scientific Analysis of the Press." *The Independent*, October 17, 1912, 896.

"Tie and Track." *Los Angeles Times*, February 8, 1890, 3.

Tinker, Fannie Palmer. "The Woman's Press Club of New York." *Chautauquan*, November 1892, 209–11.

Townsend, George Alfred. "Hearing My Requiem. [Journalist Series]." *Lippincott's Monthly Magazine*, October 1892, 494–99.

Townsend, Horace. "Interviewing as a Factor in Journalism." *North American Review*, April 1889, 522–23.

"Trade Press Association." *New York Times*, October 12, 1892, 9.

"Two Girl Heroines Save Children's Lives." *Chicago Daily Tribune*, December 23, 1899, 7.

Unit, Matthew. "Explanatory Journalism." *The Journalist*, November 21, 1885, 1.

———. "Room at the Top?" *The Journalist*, January 30, 1886, 1.

"Very Great Success, A." *The Journalist*, March 29, 1884, 6.

Walker, John Brisben. "Some Difficulties of Modern Journalism." *Cosmopolitan; a Monthly Illustrated Magazine*, January 1898, 328.

Warner, Charles Dudley. "Charles Dudley Warner Tells Some Hurting Truths of The Press." *Fourth Estate*, August 22, 1895, 5.

Watrous, A. E. "The Newspaper-Man as a Confidant. [Journalist Series]." *Lippincott's Monthly Magazine*, March 1892, 332–35.

"What Is News—Should the People Get It All?" *Newspaperdom*, June–July 1893, 127–30.

Wilcox, Delos F. "The American Newspaper: A Study in Social Psychology." *Annals of the American Academy of Political and Social Science* 16 (July 1900): 56–92.

Willis, C. W. "Newspaper Correspondence. Practical Hints and Rules by a Working Correspondent." *The Journalist*, December 13, 1890, 4.

"Women in Newspaper Work." *The New York Times*, September 6, 1894, 9.

Wood, Jessie M. "The Newspaper Woman." *Life*, May 7, 1896, 372.

"Words Not to Use." *The Journalist*, November 17, 1888, 14.

"Writing for the Press." *The Journalist*, December 15, 1888, 10.

Young, John Russell. "Men Who Reigned: Bennett, Greeley, Raymond, Prentice, Forney: [Journalist Series]." *Lippincott's Monthly Magazine*, February 1893, 185–94.

## Secondary Sources, Books & Book Chapters


Abbott, Andrew Delano. *The System of Professions: An Essay on the Division of Expert Labor.* Chicago & London: University of Chicago Press, 1988.

Adams, Bert N., and R. A. Sydie. *Sociological Theory.* Thousand Oaks, Calif.: Pine Forge Press, 2001.

Adams, Katherine H. *A History of Professional Writing Instruction in American Colleges: Years of Acceptance, Growth, and Doubt.* Dallas: Southern Methodist University Press, 1993.

Ashley, Perry J., ed. *Dictionary of Literary Biography.* Vol. 25, *American Newspaper Journalists, 1901–1925.* Detroit: Gale Research, 1984.

Baldasty, Gerald J. *The Commercialization of News in the Nineteenth Century.* Madison, Wis.: University of Wisconsin Press, 1992.

Baran, Stanley J., and Dennis K. Davis. *Mass Communication Theory: Foundations, Ferment, and Future.* 7th ed. Stamford, Conn.: Cengage Learning, 2015.

Barth, Gunther. *City People: The Rise of Modern City Culture in Nineteenth-Century America.* New York: Oxford University Press, 1980.

Berelson, Bernard. *Content Analysis in Communication Research.* 1952. Reprint, New York: Hafner Publishing Co., 1971.

Bledstein, Burton J. *The Culture of Professionalism: The Middle Class and the Development of Higher Education in America.* New York: W. W. Norton & Co., 1978.

Boyer, Paul S. *Purity in Print: Book Censorship in America from the Gilded Age to the Computer Age.* Madison: University of Wisconsin Press, 2002.

Bradley, Patricia. *Women and the Press: The Struggle for Equality.* Evanston, Ill.: Northwestern University Press, 2005.

Briefel, Aviva. *The Deceivers: Art Forgery and Identity in the Nineteenth Century.* Ithaca & London: Cornell University Press, 2006.

Burke, W. J., and Will D. Howe. *American Authors and Books, 1640–1940.* New York: Gramercy, 1943.

Canada, Mark, ed. *Literature and Journalism: Inspirations, Intersections, and Inventions from Ben Franklin to Stephen Colbert.* New York: Palgrave Macmillan, 2013.

Collins, Paul. *The Murder of the Century: The Gilded Age Crime that Scandalized a City & Sparked the Tabloid Wars.* New York: Broadway Books, 2011.

DeFleur, Melvin L. *Mass Communication Theories: Explaining Origins, Processes, and Effects.* New York: Allyn & Bacon, 2010.

Derks, Scott. *Working Americans, 1880–1999. Vol. 1, The Working Class.* Lakeville, Conn.: Grey House Publishing Inc., 2001.

———. *Working Americans, 1880–1999. Vol. 2, The Middle Class.* Millerton, N.Y.: Grey House Publishing Inc., 2001.

Dicken-Garcia, Hazel. *Journalistic Standards in Nineteenth-Century America.* Madison: University of Wisconsin Press, 1989.

Dooley, Patricia L. *Taking Their Political Place: Journalists and the Making of an Occupation.* Westport, Conn.: Greenwood Press, 1997.

———. *The Technology of Journalism: Cultural Agents, Cultural Icons.* Evanston, Ill.: Northwestern University Press, 2007.

Downs, Robert B., and Jane B. Downs. *Journalists of the United States: Biographical Sketches of Print and Broadcast News Shapers from the Late 17th Century to the Present.* Jefferson, N.C.: McFarland, 1991.

Dunbar, Robin. *How Many Friends Does One Person Need? Dunbar's Number and Other Evolutionary Quirks.* London: Faber & Faber Ltd., 2010.

Elfenbein, Julien. *Business Journalism.* 1960. Reprint, 2nd rev. ed. With a preface to the Greenwood reprint by the author. New York: Greenwood, 1969.

"Elizabeth Garver Jordan." *American National Biography.* Vol. 12, 270–71. Edited by John A. Garraty and Mark C. Carnes. New York: Oxford University Press, 1999.

Emery, Michael, Edwin Emery, and Nancy L. Roberts. *The Press and America: An Interpretive History of the Mass Media.* 9th ed. Boston: Allyn and Bacon, 2000.

Falk, Peter Hastings, ed. *Who Was Who in American Art, 1564–1975,* 3 vols. Madison, Conn.: Sound View Press, 1999.

Fedler, Fred. *Lessons from the Past: Journalists' Lives and Work, 1850–1950.* Prospect Heights, Ill.: Waveland Press, Inc., 2000.

Fishman, Mark. *Manufacturing the News.* Austin: University of Texas Press, 1980.

Gans, Herbert J. *Deciding What's News: A Study of CBS Evening News, NBC Nightly News, Newsweek, and Time.* New York: Vintage Books, 1980.

Garraty, John A., ed., and Jerome L. Sternstein, associate ed. *Encyclopedia of American Biography.* New York: Harper & Row, 1974.

Good, Howard. *Acquainted With the Night: The Image of Journalists in American Fiction, 1890–1930.* Metuchen, N.J.: The Scarecrow Press, 1986.

———. *The Journalist as Autobiographer.* Metuchen, N.J.: The Scarecrow Press, 1993.

Hale, William Harlan. *Horace Greeley: Voice of the People.* New York: Harper & Brothers, 1950.

Huntzicker, William E. *The History of American Journalism*, Vol. 3, *The Popular Press, 1833–1865*. Westport, Conn.: Greenwood Press, 1999.

"Jesse Lynch Williams," *American National Biography*. Vol. 23, 469–70. Edited by John A. Garraty and Mark C. Carnes. New York: Oxford University Press, 1999.

Johanningsmeier, Charles. *Fiction and the American Literary Marketplace: The Role of Newspaper Syndicates, 1860–1900*. New York: Cambridge University Press, 1997.

Kaniss, Phyllis C. *Making Local News*. Chicago: University of Chicago Press, 1991.

Krippendorff, Klaus. *Content Analysis: An Introduction to Its Methodology*. London & New Delhi: Sage Publications, 1980.

Kroeger, Brooke. *Nellie Bly: Daredevil, Reporter, Feminist*. New York: Times Books, 1994.

Lutes, Jean Marie. *Front-Page Girls: Women Journalists in American Culture and Fiction, 1880–1930*. Ithaca, N.Y.: Cornell University Press, 2006.

Marquis, Albert Nelson, ed. *Who's Who in America: A Biographical Dictionary of Notable Living Men and Women of the United States*. Vol. 1910–1911. Chicago: A. N. Marquis & Co., 1910.

Marzolf, Marion Tuttle. *Civilizing Voices: American Press Criticism 1880–1950*. White Plains, N.Y.: Longman, 1991.

McKerns, Joseph P., ed. *Biographical Dictionary of American Journalism*. New York: Greenwood Press, 1989.

McNair, Brian. *The Sociology of Journalism*. London & New York: Arnold, 1998.

Mott, Frank Luther. *A History of American Magazines, 1865–1885*. Vol. 3. Cambridge, Mass.: Harvard University Press, 1938.

———. *A History of American Magazines, 1885–1905*. Vol. 4. Cambridge, Mass.: Harvard University Press, 1957.

*National Cyclopedia of American Biography, 1892–1947*. Vols. 11, 18, 32. Clifton, N.J.: James T. White & Co., 1901, 1922, 1945.

O'Dell, De Forest. *The History of Journalism Education in the United States*. New York: Bureau of Publications, Teachers College, Columbia University, 1935.

O'Sullivan, John, and Edward F. Keuchel. *American Economic History: From Abundance to Constraint*. New York: Franklin Watts, 1981.

Petrik, Paula. "The Youngest Fourth Estate: The Novelty Toy Printing Press and Adolescence, 1870–1886." In *Small Worlds: Children & Adolescence in America, 1850–1950*, edited by Elliott West and Paula Petrik, 125–42. Lawrence: University Press of Kansas, 1992.

Popkin, Jeremy D. *History, Historians, and Autobiography*. Chicago: University of Chicago Press, 2005.

Quinn, Stephen. *Convergent Journalism: The Fundamentals of Multimedia Reporting*. New York: Peter Lang, 2005.

"Richard Harding Davis." *Encyclopedia of World Biography*. Vol. 4. 2nd ed., 422–23. Detroit: Gale, 2004.

Rogers, Everett M. *Diffusion of Innovations*. 5th ed. New York: Free Press, 2003.

Roggenkamp, Karen. "Elizabeth Jordan, 'True Stories of the News,' and Newspaper Fiction in Late Nineteenth-Century Journalism." In *Literature and Journalism: Inspirations, Intersections, and Inventions from Ben Franklin to Stephen Colbert*, edited by Mark Canada, 119–41. New York: Palgrave Macmillan, 2013.

Salazar, James. *Bodies of Reform: The Rhetoric of Character in Gilded Age America*. New York: New York University Press, 2010.

Salcetti, Marianne. "The Emergence of the Reporter: Mechanization and the Devaluation of Editorial Workers." In *News Workers: Toward a History of the Rank and File*, edited by Hanno Hardt and Bonnie Brennen, 48–74. Minneapolis: University of Minnesota Press, 1995.

Schudson, Michael. *The Sociology of News*. 2nd ed. New York: W. W. Norton, 2011.

Smith, Heather A., and James D. McKeen. "Creating and Facilitating Communities of Practice." In *Handbook of Knowledge Management 1: Knowledge Matters*, edited by C. W. Holsapple, 393–407. New York: Springer-Verlag, 2003.

Smythe, Ted Curtis. *The Gilded Age Press, 1865–1900*. Westport, Conn.: Praeger, 2003.

Steele, Janet E. *The Sun Shines for All: Journalism and Ideology in the Life of Charles A. Dana*. Syracuse, N.Y.: Syracuse University Press, 1993.

Stephens, Mitchell. *A History of News*. 3rd ed. New York: Oxford University Press, 2007.

Stone, Candace. *Dana and the Sun*. New York: Dodd, Mead & Co., 1938.

Tarde, Gabriel. *Gabriel Tarde on Communication and Social Influence: Selected Papers*. Edited by Terry N. Clark. Chicago & London: University of Chicago Press, 1969.

Traxel, David. *Crusader Nation: The United States in Peace and the Great War, 1898–1920*. New York: Alfred A. Knopf, 2006.

Tucher, Andie. "The True, The False, and the 'Not Exactly Lying.'" In *Literature and Journalism: Inspirations, Intersections, and Inventions from Ben Franklin to Stephen Colbert*. Edited by Mark Canada, 91–118. New York: Palgrave Macmillan, 2013.

Tuchman, Gaye. *Making News: A Study in the Construction of Reality*. New York: Free Press, 1978.

Van de Ven, Andrew H., et al. *The Innovation Journey*. New York & Oxford: Oxford University Press, 1999.

Wallace, W. Stewart. A *Dictionary of North American Authors Deceased Before 1950*. Toronto: Ryerson Press, 1951.

Weedon, Alexis. *Victorian Publishing: The Economics of Book Production for a Mass Market, 1836–1916*. Burlington, Vt.: Ashgate, 2003.

Wenger, Etienne. *Communities of Practice: Learning, Meaning and Identity*. Cambridge, U.K.: Cambridge University Press, 1998.

Whitney, D. Charles, Randall S. Sumpter, and Denis McQuail. "News Media Production: Individuals, Organizations, Institutions." In *Sage Handbook of Media Studies*, edited by J.D.H. Downing, 393–410. Thousand Oaks, Calif.: Sage Publications Inc., 2004.

*Who's Who in America*. Chicago: A. N. Marquis, 1900.

*Who Was Who in America, 1897–1942*. Vol. 1. Chicago: A. N. Marquis, 1943.

*Who Was Who Among North American Authors, 1921–1939*, 2 vols. Detroit: Gale Research Co., 1976.

*Who Was Who in Journalism, 1925–1928*. Compiled by M. N. Ask and S. Gershanek. *Gale Composite Biographical Dictionary Series*. No. 4. Detroit: Firenze, 1978.

Wilson, Christopher P. *The Labor of Words: Literary Professionalism in the Progressive Era*. Athens, Ga.: University of Georgia Press, 1985.

Wilson, Grant, and John Fiske, eds. Appleton's Cyclopaedia of American Biography. Vol. 5. New York: D. Appleton & Co., 1888.

## Secondary Sources, Articles & Newspapers

Andrews, Kenneth T., and Neal Caren. "Making the News: Movement Organizations, Media Attention, and the Public Agenda." *American Sociological Review* 75, no. 6 (2010): 841–66.

Atwood, Roy A., and Arnold S. de Beer. "The Roots of Academic News Research: Tobias Peucer's 'De relationibus Novellis (1690).'" *Journalism Studies* 2, no. 4 (2001): 485–96.

Baker, Abigail. "The Ithaca Jewel: An Authentic Fake." *Journal of the History of Collections* 28, no. 1 (2016): 97–108.

Balée, Susan. "From the Outside in: A History of American Autobiography." *Hudson Review* 51, no. 1 (spring 1998): 40–64.

Banning, Stephen A. "The Professionalization of Journalism: A Nineteenth-Century Beginning." *Journalism History* 24, no. 4 (winter 1998/1999): 157–63.

Barrera, Carlos. "Transatlantic Views on Journalism Education Before and After World War II: Two Separate Worlds?" *Journalism Studies* 13, no. 4 (2012): 534–49.

Becker, Markus C. "Organizational Routines: A Review of the Literature." *Industrial and Corporate Change* 13, no. 4 (2004): 643–78.

Bradshaw, James Stanford. "Mrs. Rayne's School of Journalism." *Journalism & Mass Communication Quarterly* 60, no. 3 (September 1983): 513–17, 579.

Breed, Warren. "Social Control in the Newsroom: A Functional Analysis." *Social Forces* 33, no. 4 (May 1955): 326–35.

Burger, Michael. "Notes and Documents: The Date and Authorship of Robert Grosseteste's Rules for Household and Estate Management." *Historical Research* 74, no. 183 (February 2001): 106–16.

Canada, Mark. "Stories of Today: Rebecca Harding Davis' Investigative Fiction." *Journalism History* 38, no. 2 (summer 2012): 63–73.

Carignan, Michael I. "Fiction as History or History as Fiction? George Eliot, Hayden White, and Nineteenth-Century Historicism." *Clio* 29, no. 4 (2000): 395–415.

Chalaby, Jean K. "No Ordinary Press Owners: Press Barons as a Weberian Ideal Type." *Media, Culture & Society* 19 (1997): 621–41.

Chubin, D. E. "Research Malpractice." *BioScience* 35 (1985): 80–89.

Clark, Justin T. "Confronting the 'Seeker of Newspaper Notoriety.' Pathological Lying, the Public, and the Press, 1890–1920." *American Journalism* 34, no. 2 (spring 2017): 179–200.

Cox, Andrew. "What Are Communities of Practice? A Comparative Review of Four Seminal Works." *Journal of Information Science* 31, no. 6 (December 2005): 527–40.

Cronin, Mary M. "Trade Press Roles in Promoting Journalistic Professionalism, 1884–1917." *Journal of Mass Media Ethics* 8, no. 4 (1993): 227–38.

Davenport, Elisabeth, and Hazel Hall. "Organizational Knowledge and Communities of Practice." *Annual Review of Information Science and Technology* 36 (2002): 171–227.

Deutsch, Claudia H. "Changing the Game with Innovations." *New York Times*, May 24, 2008, sec. C, 2.

Dimmick, John. "Sex, Violence, and the Rules of the Game: Canons and Codes as Occupational Ideologies." *Journal of Communication* 27, no. 2 (spring 1977): 181–87.

Duncan, Sallyanne, and Jackie Newton. "How Do You Feel? Preparing Novice Reporters for the Death Knock." *Journalism Practice* 4, no. 4 (2010): 439–53.

Echevarría de la Gándara, Borja. "New Challenges, New Rewards." *Nieman Reports* 67, no. 1 (spring 2013): 31–32.

Entman, R. M. "Framing: Toward Clarification of a Fractured Paradigm." *Journal of Communication* 43, no. 4 (autumn 1993): 51–58.

Farhi, Paul. "Mistaken Nation." *American Journalism Review* 34, no. 3 (winter 2012): 32–37.

Fedler, Fred. "Actions of Early Journalists Often Unethical, Even Illegal." *Journal of Mass Media Ethics* 12, no. 3 (1997): 160–70.

Frazier, P. J., and Cecilie Gaziano. "Robert Ezra Park's Theory of News, Public Opinion and Social Control." *Journalism Monographs* no. 64 (Minneapolis: Association for Education in Journalism, 1979).

García-Avilés, José Alberto. "Online Newsrooms as Communities of Practice: Exploring Digital Journalists' Applied Ethics." *Journal of Mass Media Ethics* 29 (2014): 258–72.

Goode, William J. "Community Within a Community: The Professions." *American Sociological Review* 22, no. 2 (April 1957): 194–200.

Goodhue, Norma H. "Always Look Ahead, Educator Tells Women." *Los Angeles Times*, July 17, 1955, sec. C, 2.

Gottlieb, Agnes Hooper. "Grit Your Teeth, then Learn to Swear." *American Journalism* 18, no. 1 (2001): 53–72.

Greenhalgh, Trisha, Christopher Voisey, and Nadia Robb. "Interpreted Consultations as 'Business as Usual'? An Analysis of Organizational Routines in General Practices." *Sociology of Health and Illness* 29, no. 6 (2007): 931–54.

Hoffman, Elizabeth. "'Revenge' and 'Rescue': Workplace Deviance in the Taxicab Industry." *Sociological Inquiry* 78, no. 3 (August 2008): 270–89.

Ingram, Mathew. "What a Map of the Fake-News Ecosystem Says about the Problem." *Fortune.com*, last modified November 28, 2016, http://fortune.com/2016/11/28/map-fake-news/.

Isaac, Jessica. "Youthful Enterprises: Amateur Newspapers and the Pre-History of Adolescence, 1867–1883." *American Periodicals* 22, no. 2 (2012): 158–77.

Johnson, J. David. "Influence Relationships within a Community of Practice." *Studies in Communication Sciences* 6, no. 1 (2006): 63–92.

Kaler, John. "James Otis Kaler: A Biographical Sketch." *Dime Novel Round-Up* 60, no. 6 (December 2000): 183–211.

"Kirk Munroe, Author, Dies in Miami at 69." *New York Times*, June 17, 1930, 24.

Klatt, Lawrence. "The Professionalization of Everyone." *Personnel Journal* (September 1967): 508–9, 522.

Lee, Alexander. "Portrait of the Author as a Historian." *History Today* (September 2016): 54–55.

Lindey, Sara. "Boys Write Back: Self-Education and Periodical Authorship in Late-Nineteenth-Century Story Papers." *American Periodicals* 21, no. 1 (2011): 72–78.

May, William F. "Professional Ethics, the University, and the Journalist." *Journal of Mass Media Ethics* 1, no. 2 (spring/summer 1986): 20–31.

Meriam, Lewis. "The Trend Toward Professionalization." *Annals of the American Academy of Political and Social Science* 189 (January 1937): 58–64.

Mirando, Joseph A. "Embracing Objectivity Early On: Journalism Textbooks of the 1800s." *Journal of Mass Media Ethics* 16, no. 1 (2001): 23–32.

Mitchell, Catherine. "Greeley as journalism teacher: 'give us facts, occurrences.'" *Journalism Educator* 44, no. 3 (autumn 1989): 16–19.

Nolte, Karen. "'Telling the Painful Truth'—Nurses and Physicians in the Nineteenth Century." *Nursing History Review* 16 (2008): 115–34.

Nowviskie, Bethany. "A Digital Boot Camp for Grad Students in the Humanities." *Chronicle of Higher Education* 58, no. 36 (May 4, 2012): B26–B27.

Perry, John W. "A Newspaper Visit to the 1884 Scene." *Editor & Publisher Golden Jubilee Number*, July 21, 1934, sec. 2, 292–93.

Plaisance, Patrick Lee. "A Gang of Pecksniffs Grows Up: The Evolution of Journalism Ethics Discourse in *The Journalist* and *Editor & Publisher*." *Journalism Studies* 6, no. 4 (2005): 479–91.

Pöttker, Horst. "News and Its Communicative Quality: The Inverted Pyramid—When and Why Did It Appear." *Journalism Studies* 4, no. 4 (2003): 501–11.

Putz, Peter, and Patricia Arnold. "Communities of Practice: Guidelines for the Design of Online Seminars in Higher Education." *Education, Communication & Information* 1, no. 2 (October 2001): 181–95.

Reese, Stephen D., and Jane Ballinger. "The Roots of a Sociology of News: Remembering Mr. Gates and Social Control in the Newsroom." *Journalism & Mass Communication Quarterly* 78, no. 4 (2001): 641–58.

Revers, Matthias. "Journalistic Professionalism as Performance and Boundary Work: Source Relations at the State House." *Journalism* 15, no. 1 (2014): 37–52.

Robb, Arthur. "Modern Presses Began in Eighties." *Editor & Publisher Golden Jubilee Number*, July 21, 1936, sec. 2, 198.

Rodgers, Ronald R. "'Journalism Is a Loose-Jointed Thing': A Content Analysis of *Editor & Publisher*'s Discussion of Journalistic Conduct Prior to the Canons of Journalism, 1901–1922." *Journal of Mass Media Ethics* 22, no. 1 (2007): 66–82.

Ryfe, David Michael. "The Nature of News Rules." *Political Communication* 23, no. 2 (2006): 203–14.

Sandiford, Peter, and Diane Seymour. "The Concept of Occupational Community Revisited: Analytical and Managerial Implications in Face-to-Face Service Occupations." *Work, Employment and Society* 21, no. 2 (June 2007): 209–26.

Saxon, Wolfgang. "Richard Ruopp, 65; Led Bank Street College." *The New York Times*, November 30, 1997, sec. 1, 53.

Scarbrough, Harry, and Jacky Swan. "Knowledge Communities and Innovation." *Trends in Communication* 8 (2002): 7–18.

Schudson, Michael. "The Politics of Narrative Form: The Emergence of News Conventions in Print and Television." *Daedalus* 111, no. 4 (fall 1982): 97–112.

———. "Question Authority: A History of the News Interview in American Journalism, 1860s–1930s." *Media, Culture & Society* 16, no. 4 (1994): 565–87.

Seymour, Alta Halverson. "What Can a Woman Do." *Christian Science Monitor*, November 22, 1933, 6.

Shachmurove, Yochanan. "A Historical Overview of Financial Crises in the United States." *Global Finance Journal* 22 (2011): 217–31.

Silva, Edward T., and Sheila Slaughter. "Prometheus Bound: The Limits of Social Science Professionalization in the Progressive Period." *Theory and Society* 9, no. 6 (November 1980): 781–819.

Silverman, Craig. "A New Age for Truth." *Nieman Reports* 66, no. 2 (summer 2012): 4–7.

Smith, Roland B. "The Genesis of the Business Press in the United States." *Journal of Marketing* 19, no. 2 (October 1954): 146–51.

Smythe, Ted Curtis. "The Reporter, 1880–1900. Working Conditions and Their Influence on the News." *Journalism History* 7, no. 1 (spring 1980): 1–10.

———. "The Diffusion of the Urban Daily, 1850–1900." *Journalism History* 28, no. 2 (summer 2002): 73–84.

Sobieraj, Sara. "Reporting Conventions: Journalists, Activists and the Thorny Struggle for Political Visibility." *Social Problems* 57, no. 4 (November 2010): 505–28.

Steiner, Linda. "Construction of Gender in Newsreporting Textbooks: 1890–1900." *Journalism Monographs* no. 135. Charleston, S.C.: Association for Education in Journalism and Mass Communication, 1992.

———. "Sex, Lives, and Autobiography: Contributions of Life Study to Journalism History: What Can Be Learned." *American Journalism* 13, no. 2 (1996): 206–11.

Stewart, Thomas A. "The Invisible Key to Success." *Fortune*, August 5, 1996, 173–75.

Sumpter, Randall S. "News About News: John G. Speed and the First Newspaper Content Analysis." *Journalism History* 27, no. 2 (summer 2001): 64–72.

———. "Core Knowledge: Early Reporting Textbooks and the Formation of Professional Identity." *Journalism History* 35, no. 1 (spring 2009): 42–51.

———. "Learning the 'Outsider' Profession: Serial Advice Columns in *The Journalist*." *American Journalism* 27, no. 3 (summer 2010): 7–26.

———. "'Practical Reporting': Late Nineteenth-Century Journalistic Standards and Rule Breaking." *American Journalism* 30, no. 1 (winter 2013): 44–64.

———. "'Girl Reporter': Elizabeth L. Banks and the 'Stunt' Genre." *American Journalism* 32, no. 1 (winter 2015): 60–77.

Tewksbury, Doug. "Online-Offline Knowledge Sharing in the Occupy Movement: Howtooccupy.org and Discursive Communities of Practice." *American Communication Journal* 15, no. 1 (2013): 11–23.

Thomas, Jane. "Business Writing in History: What Caused the Dictamen's Demise?" *Journal of Business Communication* 36, no. 1 (January 1999): 40–54.

Webb, Amy. "How to Make J-School Matter Again." *Nieman Reports* 69, no. 1 (winter 2015): 18–25.

Weiss, Amy Schmitz, and David Domingo. "Innovation Processes in Online Newsrooms as Actor-Networks and Communities of Practice." *New Media & Society* 12, no. 7 (2010): 1156–71.

Wenger, Etienne. "Communities of Practice and Social Learning Systems." *Organization* 7, no. 2 (2000): 225–46.

Willnat, Lars, and David H. Weaver. "The American Journalist in the Digital Age: Key Findings." Paper presented at the annual meeting of the Association for Education in Journalism and Mass Communication, Chicago, Ill., August 2017.

Winfield, Betty Houchin, and Janice Hume. "The American Hero and the Evolution of the Human Interest Story." *American Journalism* 15, no. 2 (1998): 79–99.

# Index

Note: page numbers followed by *t* refer to the table.